PASTA ITALIANA

This book is dedicated to all my fans who have been there for me from the beginning—you are truly *fantastico!*

Gino D'Acampo

PASTA ITALIANA

100 RECIPES FROM FETTUCCINE TO CONCHIGLIE

Photography by Kate Whitaker

KYLE BOOKS

Printed in 2012 by Kyle Books
www.kylebooks.com

Distributed by
National Book Network
4501 Forbes Blvd., Suite 200
Lanham, MD 20706
Phone: (800) 462-6420
Fax: (301) 429-5746
custserv@nbnbooks.com

ISBN 978-1-906868-43-7

First published in Great Britain in 2010 by
Kyle Cathie Limited

10 9 8 7 6 5 4 3 2 1

Gino D'Acampo is hereby identified as the author of this
work in accordance with Section 77 of the Copyright,
Designs, and Patents Act 1988.

Design Nicky Collings
Photography Kate Whitaker
Project Editor Vicky Orchard
Food stylist Nicole Herft
Props stylist Wei Tang
Copy editor Stephanie Evans
Production Gemma John

Library of Congress Control No: 2011937869

Color reproduction by Chromographics
Printed and bound in China by C&C Offset

Acknowledgments
A massive thank you goes to my long-term
publisher Kyle Cathie who once again trusted
me to write my fourth book.

To my manager and friend Jeremy and everybody
at Jeremy Hicks Associates for all their hard work
and commitment on all of my projects—I'm
truly grateful.

Special thanks goes to my favorite photographer
Kate Whitaker and all the team in charge who
made this book so beautiful. Vicky and Nicky—
you did a great job!

A big kiss and a big thank you goes to my food
stylist Nicole Herft and her assistant Simone for
making the food look amazing.

To everybody at Bontà Italia: Marco, Lina, Franco,
Loredana, Leo, and Graziana for their continuous
support and patience—it's great to know you're
always there for me.

Of course all this would have been impossible
without the help of my family, Luciano, Rocco, and
Jessie—thank you for making my life so beautiful.

Last but not least, a big thank you to Contessa
Maria Teresa Boselli Vespignani for providing her
beautiful villa in Italy where we shot the book.
www.agrivillelacollina.com

Grazie, grazie, grazie to you for once again
choosing my book, enjoy, and *Buon Appettito!*
www.ginodacampo.com
Twitter page—@ginofantastico

CONTENTS

INTRODUCTION

Finally it has happened... here I am writing a book dedicated exclusively to pasta—by far my favorite Italian dish ever. I remember, like it was yesterday...I was thirteen on my first day at the catering college. My teacher took me to the kitchen and showed me how to make fresh pasta dough. At that point, I got so excited that I promised myself that one day I would share this experience with as many people as possible. Since then, my love affair with pasta has never changed. If I had my way, I would eat it for breakfast, lunch, and dinner.

Growing up, I don't ever remember having a meal with my family where pasta didn't feature, especially Sunday lunch. My mother used to make, and still does, the most beautiful lasagna ever. No matter how big she made it, however, there was never any left over at the end of the meal—in fact, my sister and I used to argue over the last slice. I have carried on this tradition and most Sundays I make sure I enjoy a good plate of pasta with my wife and my boys, and it's really funny and lovely to see them, in their turn, arguing over the last serving.

Italy without pasta is like Britain without tea—it's just impossible to picture. We have more than 600 different shapes of pasta and, believe it or not, each has been designed specifically for a particular sauce. Just for the record, in Italy, there is no such thing as *spaghetti* Bolognese—we would always choose tagliatelle or pappardelle, as these absorb the flavor of the sauce much better. Of course, let's not forget all the filled pastas that we have, such as ravioli, tortelloni, and mezzelune (half-moon-shape pasta), which traditionally are always served with a light sauce (such as butter and fresh sage), mainly because you don't want the sauce to overpower the filling.

Nowadays you can buy a package of pasta from pretty much every corner store, but please trust me when I say that if you spend a little extra the end result will be 100 percent better. The best pasta is made by the traditional method of pressing the dough through a bronze die, which gives it a slightly coarse surface that allows the sauce to stick to it. This type of pasta is more expensive, but it's truly worth it!

Whichever type you choose, a plate of pasta has to be the ultimate fast-food dish. You only have to boil some salted water, cook the pasta for 7 to 8 minutes, drain, and then serve with a drizzle of extra virgin olive oil and a sprinkle of Parmesan cheese and you have a filling, tasty, healthy, and inexpensive dish—what more could you want? I can see now why there are references to macaroni dating back to the thirteenth century; also why the Chinese still maintain it was their discovery. Rubbish! Pasta has to be, and certainly was, the creation of an Italian.

In this book, you will find 100 tasty, stylish, yet very simple pasta recipes that can be used for a quick meal or as a course for your dinner party. All the ingredients are widely available, which means you won't need to drive yourself mad finding them. I have also chosen dishes that can be served to children and adults at the same time, just to make dinner a little easier.

All of them demonstrate that you don't need to spend a lot of time in the kitchen to enjoy a great Italian dish and will tell you everything you need to know about cooking the perfect plate of pasta. Of course, *Pasta Italiana* is perfect for my ongoing motto too:

Minimum Effort, Maximum Satisfaction!

Buon Appetito!

THE NUTRITIONAL BENEFITS OF PASTA

By Juliette Kellow BSc RD

Carbohydrate-rich foods like pasta, rice, bread, couscous, and potatoes have had a hard time in recent years. For a while, the popularity of low-carb slimming diets turned a delicious plate of spaghetti into the enemy. But fortunately, thanks to continued scientific research, health experts remain convinced that carbs are more friend than foe when it comes to keeping us healthy and staying in shape—providing we choose the right sort and don't eat them in enormous portions.

Of course, it's something true Italians have always known. Screen legend and Hollywood beauty Sophia Loren famously claimed that eating pasta helped to contribute

to her youthful looks. "Everything you see, I owe to spaghetti," she once said. Meanwhile, in her book *Women & Beauty*, she states, "Italians are lucky to live with a culinary heritage that relies on pasta because it is a complex carbohydrate and a very efficient and healthy fuel for the body."

Health experts agree. In the US, the Department of Health and Human Services (HHS) and the Department of Agriculture (USDA) maintain that starchy foods like pasta are an important part of a healthy, balanced diet and recommend that they make up roughly a third of the food we eat. Omitting starchy foods from our diet can be

bad for our health because we could miss out on a range of vital nutrients, and it could also reduce our daily intake of valuble dietary fiber, which may help to reduce the risk of cancer.

Other countries in the Western world are of the same opinion. Health guidelines throughout Europe, Australia, and New Zealand recommend that starchy foods, together with fruits and vegetables, form the majority of our diet.

Meanwhile, the idea that carbs like pasta are "fattening" is something of a myth. Basically, it's an excess of calories that makes us pile on the pounds—and it really doesn't matter where these extra calories come from. There's certainly no good evidence to suggest that carbs are solely responsible for the nation's expanding waistlines— or that, if we want to lose weight, a low-carb diet is the best way to achieve it. Indeed, research shows that in the long term, there's no significant difference in the amount of weight lost by people following either a low-carbohydrate or low-calorie diet.

Furthermore, carbs actually contain half the calories of fat—a gram of pure carbohydrate provides just 4 calories, compared to 9 calories in a gram of pure fat! Ultimately, it's what you serve carbs with that can pile on the calories. More often than not, the fat we add to carbs is what boosts the calorie content. For example, an 8 ounce serving of cooked spaghetti contains just 239 calories. Mixing it with 2 tablespoons olive oil adds an extra 200 calories— almost doubling the calories of the dish.

PASTA PERFECTION FOR WAISTLINES

When it comes to choosing which carbs to eat, pasta is a great choice. Like many other starchy foods, pasta is naturally low in fat and saturated fat, and is an important source of energy. But—unlike some other carbs—it releases its energy slowly and steadily, thanks to its low glycemic index, or GI. The glycemic index measures the effect different carbohydrate-containing foods have on our blood sugar levels. Foods with a low GI release sugar into the blood slowly, providing us with a steady supply of energy that leaves us satisfied for longer and so less likely to snack. By contrast, foods with a high GI cause a rapid, but short-lived, rise in blood sugar followed by a sudden crash. As a result, we quickly feel low on energy and hungry again, meaning that we're more likely to snack, especially on sugary foods, to give us a quick boost. Over time, this frequent snacking can lead to unwanted weight gain. Health experts agree that it's better to choose a diet that contains carbohydrate-rich foods with a low to medium GI because they help to keep us fuller for longer.

It's good news then that pasta has a lower GI than many other starchy foods that are traditionally eaten as an accompaniment to entrees. According to the GI scale, both white and whole-wheat varieties of pasta

COOK "AL DENTE"
To help ensure pasta keeps us full for as long as possible, it's important to avoid overcooking it. The reason pasta has such a low GI is because the starch granules become "trapped" in the pasta dough when it is made. Cooking starts to release these starch granules, making it easier for the body's digestive processes to break them down into sugars. More of the starches remain "trapped" in pasta that is cooked for a shorter time, which is why Gino stresses you cook your pasta so it is al dente or "firm to the bite." As a result, lightly cooked pasta makes the digestive system work harder to break the starches into sugars, which in turn slows the release of these sugars into the bloodstream. Ultimately, al dente pasta has a lower GI than soft, soggy pasta that's been overcooked, and so will help to stave off any hunger pangs to keep you feeling fuller for longer. As a rule of thumb, try cooking your pasta for one minute less than the package directions recommend.

are classified as having a low GI. In comparison, boiled potatoes, basmati and brown rice, and couscous have a medium GI, while mashed and baked potatoes, white and whole-wheat bread, and white rice all have a high GI. Bottom line: pasta is likely to keep us feeling satisfied and fuller for longer than many other popular starchy foods, making it easier for us to control our weight—and lose any excess pounds if necessary.

But foods with a low GI don't just help us to keep our waistlines in good shape. Many studies have revealed that diets containing plenty of low-GI foods may also help to protect us from a range of diseases. Australian scientists, for example, recently reviewed 37 studies that had looked at low-GI diets and the risk of chronic disease. In 2008, they published their findings in the *American Journal of Clinical Nutrition* and concluded that people with the lowest GI diets were the least likely to suffer from type 2

HEALTHY PASTA LEFTOVERS

Storing leftover pasta in the refrigerator overnight and using it to make a pasta salad for lunch the next day is a great way to further lower its GI. This is because the cooking and cooling process alters the structure of the starch in the pasta, causing some of it to resist digestion. This "resistant starch" is not digested and so doesn't break down into its component sugars. This means cooked-and-quickly-cooled pasta has less impact on our blood sugar levels and so has an even lower GI than pasta eaten immediately after cooking. Resistant starch passes into the large intestine where it provides "food" for good bacteria, which help to keep our immune and digestive systems in good working order.

diabetes, coronary heart disease, gall-bladder disease, and breast cancer.

WHOLE-WHEAT GOODNESS

While all pasta is low in fat and a good source of starchy carbs, as the chart shows, whole-wheat pasta is a richer source of fiber and nutrients than white pasta. This is because it is made from the whole of the wheat grain, including the nutrient-rich germ, the energy-providing endosperm, and the fiber-rich bran layer. When wheat grains are refined, the outer bran layer and germ of the grain are stripped away, so the grain loses much of its fiber and many of its vitamins, minerals, and antioxidants. Together with starchy carbohydrates, it is this package of nutrients in whole-grain foods such as whole-wheat pasta that is thought to be linked to good health.

Pasta Nutrition Know-How

Nutrient	Cooked white spaghetti (per 8-ounce serving)	Recommended intakes for adults (%)	Cooked whole-wheat spaghetti (per 8-ounce serving)	Recommended intakes for adults (%)
Energy (kcal)	239	12	260	13
Protein (g)	8.3	18	10.8	24
Fat (g)	1.6	2	2.1	3
Of which saturates (g)	0.2	1	0.2	1
Carbohydrates (g)	51.1	22	53.4	23
Of which sugars (g)	1.2	1	3	3
Fiber (g)	2.8	16	8.1	45
Salt (g)	0	0	0.1	2
Minerals				
Potassium (mg)	55	3	322	16
Magnesium (mg)	35	9	97	26
Phosphorus (mg)	101	14	253	36
Iron (mg)	1.2	9	3.2	23
Copper (mg)	0.2	20	0.4	40
Zinc (mg)	1.2	12	2.5	25
Manganese (mg)	0.7	35	2.1	105
Vitamins				
Thiamin (mg)	0.02	2	0.48	44
Niacin equivalents (mg)	2.8	18	5.3	33

A typical serving of whole-wheat spaghetti contains almost three times the fiber of white spaghetti and provides almost half the recommended daily fiber intake for adults.

In fact, many studies have shown that whole-grain foods can help to keep us slim and protect us from disease. For example, in one study that looked at the diets of more than 74,000 female nurses over a 12-year period, the women who ate the most whole grains consistently weighed less than those who ate the least—and were half as likely to gain weight. There's also good evidence to suggest that adults who eat more whole-grain foods are less likely to suffer with insulin resistance (a precursor for type 2 diabetes) and heart disease. Other research shows that a good, regular intake of whole grains helps to keep the digestive system healthy, prevents gallstones, and reduces the risk of developing breast and colon cancer.

A PERFECT PARTNER

Pasta provides a fantastic foundation for putting together a balanced, nutritious meal. To help people create healthy meals, most health organizations throughout the Western world recommend eating fewer fatty and sugary foods, in favor of choosing most of our food intake from the following groups:

• Starchy foods such as pasta, bread, rice, and potatoes
• Fruits and vegetables
• Protein-rich foods such as meat, fish, eggs, and beans
• Dairy products such as milk, cheese, and yogurt

Using pasta as the base for meals, it is easy to add ingredients from each of the other main food groups. For example, serving pasta with a classic Bolognese sauce that

KEY NUTRIENTS IN PASTA

Potassium—Potassium works with sodium to control the balance of fluids in the body. It is also needed to conduct nerve impulses and initiate muscle contractions, as well as to regulate heartbeat and blood pressure.

Magnesium—This mineral clots blood and is needed for strong bones and teeth. It is involved in energy production, nerve function, and muscle relaxation, and helps to regulate the rhythm of the heart.

Phosphorus—Phosphorus is needed for strong bones and teeth, and is important for energy production and healthy cells.

Iron—Iron is needed for healthy blood, is a component of many enzymes, and helps keep the immune system healthy.

Copper—This nutrient is important for immunity and keeping the heart healthy. It is also a component of collagen—a protein in bones, skin, and connective tissue.

Zinc—Zinc is essential for normal growth, enzyme function, wound healing, fertility, and for keeping the immune system strong to fight infection.

Manganese—Manganese is important for healthy bones and brain function, and is needed to produce sex hormones.

Vitamin B1 (thiamin)—This vitamin releases the energy from nutrients, keeps the heart healthy, and is essential for a healthy nervous system, growth in children, and fertility in adults.

Vitamin B3 (niacin)—This vitamin also releases the energy from nutrients and helps to control blood sugar levels. It keeps skin healthy and ensures the nervous and digestive systems function properly.

PASTA DO'S AND DON'TS

Don't...

- Overcook pasta—keep it "al dente" to keep the GI low
- Discard leftover pasta—cold pasta has a lower GI than hot pasta and is perfect for making salads
- Add too much salt to the cooking water—health experts say adults should have no more than 6g salt a day
- Use oil in the cooking water—as well as adding extra calories and fat, it means your sauce won't stick to the surface of the pasta as easily

Do...

- Choose your sauce wisely—for a healthy meal, opt for a low-fat sauce such as a classic tomato sauce made from a little olive oil, onions, garlic, herbs, and tomatoes
- Try whole-wheat pasta—it now comes in lots of different varieties, including penne, fusilli, and spaghetti
- Add lots of vegetables to pasta—or include them in sauces
- Stick to sensible portions— no more than 8 ounces cooked (3½ ounces uncooked)

Indeed, many of the recipes in this book are great examples of how pasta-based meals can help us to eat more veggies in a tasty way. Each serving of Gino's Tagliatelle Primavera (see page 33) provides two of your 5-a-day—add a salad and you're more than halfway there!

Pasta is also a great choice for people who follow a vegetarian diet—protein-rich alternatives to meat and fish, such as beans and nuts, are perfect for partnering with pasta in a sauce or salad. Finally, even people with an intolerance to wheat or gluten can enjoy pasta these days, thanks to an increasingly wide range of pastas based on corn, rice, and even quinoa (see the last chapter).

includes tomatoes, mushrooms, and carrots (from fruit and vegetables), and lean ground beef (from protein-rich foods), topped off with a sprinkling of Parmesan (from dairy products), provides a well-balanced, nutritious meal that is in line with the healthy-eating guidelines of most countries in the West.

In particular, pasta is a great vehicle for adding more vegetables to our diet, helping us to achieve our 5-a-day. A whole host of vegetables can be added to (or hidden in!) pasta sauces—especially good news for fussy eaters who love pasta but are less keen on eating vegetables.

GINO'S TIPS FOR PERFECT PASTA

The most common question I get asked about cooking pasta is if there is ever any need to add oil to the boiling water. The answer is very simple: NEVER drizzle oil into the water when you cook pasta—it's a waste of both time and money. Oil is lighter than water and therefore when you add it to the boiling water it rises to the surface, so it doesn't prevent the pasta sticking together because the pasta stays below it.

What will help the pasta not to stick to each other is the bubbles in the boiling water that continuously move the pasta around the pan. Make sure you always have a large pan when you are cooking pasta—I would usually suggest a 9 1/2-inch-diameter pot at least 8 inches tall, which will enable you to cook 2 1/4 pounds pasta at a time.

You should never cook more than 2 1/4 pounds pasta at a time, otherwise it can be difficult to prevent it sticking together. For every 18 ounces dried or fresh pasta, you need 5 quarts water, and for every 5 quarts water you will need 2 heaping tablespoons salt. Of course, remember if you are making a sauce that will make the pasta more salty, such as one using anchovies, capers, or olives, you won't need as much salt in the boiling water, so perhaps cut to 1 heaping tablespoon instead.

In my family we always calculate 4 1/4 ounces dried pasta per serving—therefore, we usually use an 18-ounce package for four people. Of course you can use less, but more would be very greedy.

If I had to choose the best tools to cook a great pasta dish they would be :

- **A large pot**
- **A large colander/strainer** for draining the cooked pasta
- **A long pair of tongs**, which are useful for any long-shape pasta
- **A long wooden spoon**, which can be used to stir the pasta and the sauce you are preparing.
- **A large skillet or sauté pan, or saucepan** to make the sauce—it's important to allow the sauce to coat the pasta before serving it and you therefore need enough space to stir them together comfortably.

Cooking the pasta in a pot of boiling water with the lid on can be another common mistake, simply because eventually the water will overflow, making a big mess in your kitchen. If you want to achieve the perfect al dente bite, cook the pasta for one minute less than directed on the package.

One of the biggest secrets to making a perfect plate of pasta is to make sure the sauce is ready before you start cooking the pasta, otherwise the pasta will be cooked and start to become soggy while waiting for the sauce to cook.

There are more than 600 different varieties of pasta and in Italy we use each shape with a specific sauce, for example farfalline (little bows), diatalini (little fingers), and stelline (little stars) are used mainly in soups, as they are smaller. Linguine is used with seafood sauces and farfalle, macaroni, tagliatelle, and fettuccine are usually accompanied with traditional tomato-based sauces. If you like creamy sauces, make sure you use a pasta with ridges like penne rigate or fusilli so the sauce sticks to the pasta.

If you are making filled pasta, such as ravioli, mezzelune, or tortelloni, remember you can freeze it. Simply place a single layer of the filled pasta on a tray sprinkled with flour or semolina and place in the freezer, making sure they don't touch one another while they freeze. Once frozen, the shapes can be put in plastic bags and stored for up to five months. To cook the frozen pasta, allow a minute longer than usual, as the heat of the water needs to pass into the frozen fillings.

GINO'S **TOP TEN PASTA TIPS**

1 To cook the perfect pasta, you should always make sure you have enough water in the pot. You need about 5 quarts water to cook 18 ounces pasta.

2 Make sure the water is always *bollente* (fast boiling) before you start cooking the pasta.

3 For every 5 quarts water you will need 2 heaping tablespoons salt.

4 Never ever cook pasta with the lid on the pot.

5 Stir the pasta into the boiling water at least every 2 minutes during cooking.

6 There is never any need to put oil into the boiling water before you cook the pasta—it's just a waste of time and money.

7 Make sure the pasta is always cooked al dente (firm to the bite)—so keep tasting as you cook.

8 Remember fresh pasta always cooks faster than dried varieties.

9 When making pasta dough, make sure you don't overknead it, otherwise the dough will become warm and more difficult to stretch.

10 The most important rule of all—always make sure the pasta is coated in the sauce and never just pile the sauce on top of the pasta.

FRESH & FILLED PASTA

MAKING PASTA
Homemade egg pasta dough

I know you may think this is complicated and challenging, but please promise me that at some point you will try it. I can assure you, when you've made your fresh pasta dough once, you will definitely do it again. You really will feel satisfied making a dish completely from scratch—have a go and you won't be disappointed.

Makes about 14 ounces
2 ⅓ cups white flour, type "00," plus extra for dusting
3 medium eggs
½ teaspoon fine salt
1 tablespoon extra virgin olive oil

1 Sift the flour onto your counter. Make a well in the center and break in the eggs. Add in the salt and oil.

2 Using the handle of a wooden spoon, mix the flour into the eggs, working from the center outward. Once you have a crumbly texture, gather the mixture together with your hands and start to knead until you have a soft dough.

3 Once the dough has come together, continue to knead for about 8 minutes, using both hands, exactly as if you were kneading bread.

4 Roll the dough into a ball, cover with plastic wrap, and let rest in the refrigerator for 20 minutes.

5 Once the dough has rested, simply flatten it with your fingers so that the dough can fit through the rollers of the pasta machine.

6 Flour the pasta lightly on both sides and start to roll it through the pasta machine from the widest setting to the thinnest. Make sure you keep the pasta dusted with flour at all times.

VARIATIONS
Green pasta: Cook 8 ounces fresh spinach, drain thoroughly, and then blend in a food processor. Add with the eggs.

Tomato pasta: Add 2 tablespoons tomato paste with the eggs.

FRESH EGG TAGLIATELLE

Makes about 14 ounces

1 Prepare the dough as described on page 19 and remove from the refrigerator after resting.

2 Once the dough has rested, simply flatten it with your fingers so that the dough can fit through the rollers of the pasta machine.

3 Flour the pasta lightly on both sides and start to roll it through the pasta machine from the widest setting to the thinnest. Make sure you keep the pasta dusted with flour at all times. Then roll the pasta through the tagliatelle cutting attachment, gently lifting the strands as you do so.

4 If you don't have a pasta machine you can cut the tagliatelle by hand. Dust the counter, the dough, and the rolling pin with flour to prevent sticking.

5 Start by flattening the dough with the palm of your hand, then place the rolling pin across the dough and roll it toward the center. Continue to roll the pin back and forth turning the dough every so often.

6 At this point the dough should spread out and flatten evenly. When it is thin enough to see your fingers through it, it's ready.

7 Start to fold the pasta sheet like a flattened cigar from one edge to the center, and then repeat from the other edge to the center.

8 Use a well-floured, long sharp knife to cut the rolled dough into $1/4$-inch-wide strips.

9 Slide the knife beneath the rolled pasta sheet, lining up the edge of the knife with the center of the folds. Gently lift up the knife and the pasta will fall down on each side.

10 Toss the tagliatelle in a little more flour and cook within the hour.

PAPPARDELLE ALLO ZAFFERANO
Fresh saffron pappardelle

The earthy flavor of the saffron mixed into the pasta dough is a delicious combination. It will make your pasta very, very yellow, which will add to the look as well as the taste. Make sure you don't overknead the dough, otherwise it will become warm and therefore difficult to stretch into the pasta machine.

Makes about 14 ounces
3 medium eggs
6 x 0.125g sachets saffron powder
2⅓ cups white flour, type "00," plus extra for dusting
½ teaspoon fine salt
1 tablespoon extra virgin olive oil

1 In a medium-size bowl, beat the eggs lightly with the saffron powder.

2 Sift the flour into a large bowl. Make a well in the center and add the beaten eggs, salt, and oil.

3 Using the handle of a wooden spoon, mix the flour into the eggs, working from the center outward. Once you have a crumbly texture, turn the mixture out onto a well-floured counter and start to knead until you have a soft dough.

4 Once the dough has come together, continue to knead for about 8 minutes using both hands, exactly as if you were kneading bread.

5 Roll the dough into a ball, cover with plastic wrap, and let rest in the refrigerator for 20 minutes.

6 Dust the counter, the dough, and the rolling pin with flour to prevent sticking.

7 Start by flattening the dough with the palm of your hand, then place the rolling pin across the dough and roll it toward the center. Continue to roll the pin back and forth, turning the dough every so often.

8 At this point the dough should spread out and flatten evenly. When it is thin enough to see your fingers through it, it's ready.

9 Start to fold the pasta sheet like a flattened cigar from one edge to the center, and then repeat from the other edge to the center.

10 Use a long sharp knife to cut the rolled dough into ⅝-inch-wide strips.

11 Slide the knife beneath the rolled pasta sheet, lining up the edge of the knife with the center of the folds.

12 Gently lift up the knife and the pasta ribbons will fall down on each side.

13 Toss the pappardelle in a little more flour and cook within the hour.

14 Cook in a large pot of boiling salted water for 2 to 3 minutes until al dente.

MEZZELUNE DI ZUCCA E NOCI
Pasta filled with roasted butternut squash and walnuts

This has to be the queen of all filled pasta. The combination of butternut squash with walnuts and thyme is absolutely lovely. If you prefer, you can substitute the walnuts with pine nuts, and make sure you use a good-quality Italian extra virgin olive oil to drizzle over the pasta.

Serves 6

14 ounces fresh egg pasta dough, see page 19

2 eggs, beaten
¾ cup plus 1 tablespoon extra virgin olive oil
1 cup freshly grated Parmesan cheese

For the filling
1 butternut squash, about 1½ pounds
3 tablespoons extra virgin olive oil
4 tablespoons finely chopped walnuts
3 tablespoons freshly grated Parmesan cheese
3 tablespoons finely chopped raisins
2 tablespoons finely chopped fresh thyme leaves,
  plus extra to serve
salt and pepper to taste

1 Preheat the oven to 400°F.

2 First make the filling: Peel the butternut squash, cut in half, and remove the seeds and fibers. Chop into 1¼-inch cubes and place on a baking sheet.

3 Drizzle with the 3 tablespoons extra virgin olive oil and roast in the oven for 1 hour until soft and colored. Remove from the oven and let cool. Place the squash in a food processor and blend until creamy. Pour the purée into a strainer and let stand to allow any excess water to drain, 1 hour. Transfer to a bowl and fold in the remaining ingredients for the filling. Season with salt and pepper.

4 Gradually roll the dough out in a pasta machine to its thinnest setting. Make sure you continuously dust the sheets with a little flour, otherwise they can get sticky.

5 Lay the pasta sheets on a well-floured counter and then cut into circles using a 3¼-inch cutter—you should get 28 to 30.

6 Place about a teaspoonful of filling in the center of each circle, sharing it out equally. Brush the edges of the circles with beaten egg and fold over to make half-moon shapes. Press down to seal with your fingertips. Using a fork, press the edges again to secure the filling.

7 Cook the mezzelune in a large pot of boiling salted water for 1 minute (work in batches if necessary), drain, and place in the center of a large serving plate.

8 Season with a little salt and pepper. Drizzle with the extra virgin olive oil, sprinkle with the Parmesan and a little extra thyme, and serve immediately.

FETTUCCINE AL RAGÙ

Fettuccine with meat and red wine sauce

A traditional Italian ragù sauce will take you a good twenty hours of cooking and you will need more than twenty-five ingredients to prepare it. This is not the case for this recipe, but trust me, there is no compromise as far as flavors are concerned. If you prefer you can substitute the ground pork with lamb for a variation.

Serves 6

4 tablespoons olive oil

1 onion, peeled and finely chopped

1 large carrot, peeled and grated

2 celery stalks, finely chopped

18 ounces ground beef

18 ounces ground pork

salt and pepper to taste

2 glasses of dry red wine

2¾ cups strained tomatoes

2 tablespoons tomato paste

¾ cup plus 1 tablespoon chicken stock

18 ounces fresh fettuccine or egg tagliatelle, see page 21

1 In a large saucepan, heat the olive oil and cook the onion, carrot, and celery over medium heat for 5 minutes, stirring occasionally with a wooden spoon.

2 Add the ground meats and cook, stirring continuously, until colored all over, 5 minutes. Season to taste with salt and pepper.

3 Pour in the wine, stir well, and cook until the wine has evaporated, 5 minutes.

4 Pour in the strained tomatoes with the tomato paste and the stock, lower the heat, and cook, uncovered, for

2 hours. Stir every 20 minutes to prevent sticking.

5 Once the sauce is ready, remove from the heat, season with salt and pepper, and set aside.

6 Cook the pasta in a large pot of boiling salted water until al dente. Drain and return to the same pan.

7 Place the pasta pan back over low heat, pour in the ragù sauce, and gently stir everything together for 30 seconds to allow the flavors to combine.

8 Serve hot.

TAGLIATELLE CON GAMBERI E BRANDY
Tagliatelle with shrimp and a creamy brandy sauce

This is the ideal plate of pasta for a first date or if you need to be forgiven. It's delicate, full of flavors, and very impressive. You can substitute the brandy with Marsala wine and please make sure you don't overcook the shrimp.

Serves 4

2 tablespoons salted butter
4 tablespoons olive oil
2 shallots, peeled and finely chopped
1/2 cup chopped walnuts
11 ounces raw medium shrimp, peeled
10 cherry tomatoes, quartered
salt and pepper to taste
1/4 cup brandy
1 heaping cup heavy cream
1 tablespoon balsamic vinegar
14 ounces fresh egg tagliatelle, see page 21
2 tablespoons freshly chopped flat-leaf parsley

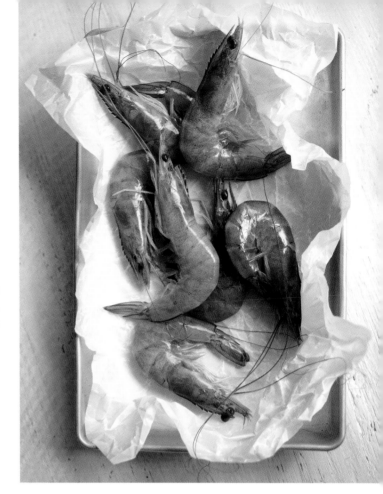

1 In a large skillet, melt the butter with the oil over low heat and sauté the shallots and walnuts for 2 minutes, stirring occasionally with a wooden spoon.

2 Increase the heat to medium, add the shrimp and tomatoes, season with salt and pepper, and cook for an additional 30 seconds.

3 Pour in the brandy and cook for 1 minute more to allow the alcohol to evporate.

4 Add the cream with the balsamic vinegar and cook, stirring, for 2 minutes. Set aside.

5 Meanwhile, cook the pasta in a large pot of boiling salted water until al dente. Drain and add back into the same pan.

6 Pour in the cream sauce with the parsley and toss everything together for 30 seconds to allow the flavors to combine.

7 Serve immediately.

FETTUCCINE CON POLLO E DOLCELATTE
Fettuccine with chicken and Dolcelatte

On Italian menus there is often an option of baked penne with a creamy chicken sauce. From this I created what I feel is the ultimate chicken pasta. Adding the wine, chives, and Dolcelatte gives the meat an amazing flavor and pairing it with fettuccine works brilliantly. It's a really hearty meal and will leave you completely satisfied. If you can't find Dolcelatte, you can substitute Gorgonzola.

Serves 4

2 tablespoons olive oil
12 ounces boneless and skinless chicken breast, cut into thin strips
7 ounces Dolcelatte cheese, cut into chunks
2/3 cup heavy cream
3 tablespoons dry white wine
3 tablespoons freshly chopped chives
salt and pepper to taste
14 ounces fresh fettuccine or egg tagliatelle, see page 21

1 In a medium saucepan, heat the oil over medium heat and sauté the chicken, stirring occasionally with a wooden spoon, until golden all over, 6 minutes. Add the Dolcelatte to the pan, lower the heat, and cook, stirring, until melted, 2 minutes.

2 Pour in the cream and wine and cook for an additional minute, stirring continuously.

3 Mix in the chives and season with salt and plenty of black pepper. Set aside.

4 Meanwhile, cook the pasta in a large pot of boiling salted water until al dente. Drain and add back into the same pan.

5 Pour in the sauce and stir everything together for 30 seconds to allow the sauce to coat the pasta evenly.

6 Serve immediately.

TAGLIATELLE PRIMAVERA

Spicy tagliatelle with bell peppers, zucchini, red onions, and thyme

I never want to hear from anyone that it's hard to cook for a vegetarian. I know if you are a meat lover it can be annoying, but there are some amazing meat-free pasta dishes out there you can cook and this is one of them. Bell peppers, zucchini, and onions are a great combination of vegetables and with a small punch of chile make this meal delicious. You can substitute fettuccine for tagliatelle if you prefer, and make sure you don't overcook the vegetables.

Serves 4

8 tablespoons olive oil
2 red onions, peeled and finely sliced
**2 yellow bell peppers, halved, seeded, and chopped
  into 1/2-inch cubes**
**1 red bell pepper, halved, seeded, and chopped
  into 1/2-inch cubes**
1 zucchini, trimmed and chopped into 1/2-inch cubes
1/2 teaspoon red pepper flakes
1 tablespoon fresh thyme leaves
salt to taste
14 ounces fresh egg tagliatelle, see page 21

1 In a large skillet, heat the oil over medium heat and sauté the onions, bell peppers, zucchini, red pepper flakes, and thyme for 8 minutes, stirring occasionally with a wooden spoon. Season with salt and set aside.

2 Meanwhile, cook the pasta in a large pot of boiling salted water until al dente. Drain and return to the same pan.

3 Pour in the sauce, place the pan over low heat, and toss everything together for 30 seconds to allow the flavors to combine.

4 Divide the pasta among four serving plates and then serve immediately.

TAGLIATELLE IN SALSA TARTARA
Tagliatelle in creamy tartare sauce

For anyone like me who loves the flavor of pickled gherkins, onions, and capers, this is definitely the pasta dish for you. Of course my inspiration came from the famous tartare sauce to which a little heavy cream is added—it works beautifully with fresh tagliatelle. You can substitute the tagliatelle with spaghetti or linguine if you prefer, but please make sure they are cooked al dente.

Serves 4
1/3 cup small pickled onions
heaping 1/3 cup small pickled gherkins
4 tablespoons salted capers, rinsed under cold water
2 tablespoons salted butter
2/3 cup heavy cream
1 teaspoon English mustard
salt and pepper to taste
14 ounces fresh egg tagliatelle, see page 21
2 egg yolks
4 tablespoons freshly chopped flat-leaf parsley
4 tablespoons freshly grated Parmesan cheese

1 Pat the onions and gherkins dry of their vinegar and place on a cutting board with the capers. Coarsely chop.

2 In a large skillet, melt the butter over medium heat and sauté the chopped onions, gherkins, and capers together for 2 minutes.

3 Pour in the cream and mustard, mix well, and cook gently for an additional 3 minutes. Season with salt and pepper and stir occasionally.

4 Meanwhile, cook the pasta in a large pot of boiling salted water until al dente.

5 Drain and add to the skillet with the creamy sauce. Add the egg yolks and sprinkle in the parsley. Toss everything together over low heat for 15 seconds to allow the sauce to coat the pasta.

6 Divide the pasta among four serving plates and serve immediately, topped with the Parmesan cheese.

FETTUCCINE ALLE CIPOLLE

Fettuccine with sweet onions, rosemary, and ground lamb

I am begging you to try this one—it's a must! This recipe is so easy to prepare—adding in the wine and stock gives the lamb such a lovely flavor and the onions create a truly creamy texture. Even thinking about this dish makes my mouth water. In fact, I paused through writing this intro to make this very dish. Think roast lamb with fresh rosemary, sautéed onions, and a glass of wine. Imagine those flavors and now add pasta—heaven.

Serves 4

6 tablespoons olive oil
3 large onions, peeled and finely sliced
1 carrot, peeled and finely grated
1 tablespoon freshly chopped rosemary
7 ounces ground lamb
3/4 cup plus 1 tablespoon white wine
salt and pepper to taste
1 1/4 cups vegetable stock
14 ounces fresh fettuccine or egg tagliatelle, see page 21
1 cup freshly grated Parmesan cheese

1 In a large saucepan, heat the olive oil and sauté the onions, carrot, and rosemary over medium heat, stirring occasionally with a wooden spoon, until softened and golden, 5 minutes.

2 Add the lamb and mix well, allowing the meat to crumble. Cook, stirring frequently, until the meat has browned all over, 5 minutes.

3 Pour in the wine and cook for another 3 minutes to allow the alcohol to evaporate. Season with salt and pepper and pour in the stock. Bring to a boil, then lower the heat and simmer, uncovered, for 30 minutes. Stir every 10 minutes.

4 Meanwhile, cook the pasta in a large pot of boiling salted water until al dente.

5 Drain the pasta and immediately add to the meat sauce. Increase the heat to high and gently mix the sauce and the pasta together for 30 seconds, stirring continuously, to allow the sauce to coat the pasta evenly.

6 Serve immediately, topped with the freshly grated Parmesan cheese.

MEZZELUNE CON PROSCIUTTO E POMODORI SECCHI
Half-moon-shape pasta filled with ham and sun-dried tomatoes

In the D'Acampo family we adore making fresh filled pasta and this recipe is one of our top ten must-have meals. If you wish, substitute the cooked ham with prosciutto.

Serves 6
3/4 cup plus 1 tablespoon extra virgin olive oil
7 ounces chorizo, cut into 1/4-inch slices
14 ounces fresh egg pasta dough, see page 19
2 eggs, beaten
3 1/2-ounce piece of Pecorino cheese, shaved

For the filling
3 cups ricotta cheese
1 1/2 cups finely chopped cooked ham
3/4 cup sun-dried tomatoes in oil, drained and chopped
15 fresh basil leaves, chopped
1 cup freshly grated Pecorino cheese
salt and pepper to taste

1 In a large bowl, mix all the ingredients for the filling together using a fork. Season with salt and pepper. Cover with plastic wrap and let rest in the refrigerator for 10 minutes.

2 Meanwhile, in a skillet, heat the extra virgin olive oil over medium heat and cook the chorizo for 3 minutes, stirring occasionally. Set aside.

3 Flatten the prepared pasta dough with your fingers so that it can fit through the rollers of the pasta machine. Flour the pasta lightly on both sides and start to roll it from the widest setting to the thinnest. Make sure you keep the pasta dusted with flour at all times.

4 Lay the pasta sheets on a well-floured counter. Cut into circles using a 3 1/4-inch cutter—you should get 28 to 30 circles. Place about a teaspoonful of filling in the center of each circle, sharing it out equally. Brush the edges of the circles with beaten egg and fold over to make half-moon shapes. Press down to seal with your fingertips. Using a fork, press the edges again to secure the filling.

5 Cook the mezzelune in a large pot of boiling salted water for 1 minute (work in batches if necessary), drain, and place in the center of a large serving plate. Season with a little salt and pepper.

6 Top with the chorizo and its oil, sprinkle with the Pecorino shavings, and serve immediately.

TAGLIATELLE
AL TARTUFO
Tagliatelle served with butter and truffle shavings

I have to admit that this is probably the most expensive recipe in this book, as I'm using the most luxurious ingredient you can buy—truffle. My best friend Marco is obsessed with this plate of pasta and of course whenever I have the chance to make it he always gets the first invite. Whatever you do, make sure you never buy truffle preserved in brine. You must only use fresh truffle, otherwise please don't try this recipe because you will be disappointed.

Serves 4

1/3 cup salted butter
salt and pepper to taste
14 ounces fresh egg tagliatelle, see page 21
1 small fresh white or black truffle
2/3 cup freshly grated Parmesan cheese

1 In a large skillet, melt the butter with plenty of black pepper. Set aside.

2 Meanwhile, cook the pasta in a large pot of boiling salted water until al dente. Drain and add to the skillet with the butter. Season with salt and toss together for 10 seconds, allowing the butter to coat the pasta evenly.

3 Divide the tagliatelle among four serving plates and shave the fresh truffle on top.

4 Sprinkle the top with the grated Parmesan cheese and serve immediately.

RAVIOLI CON RICOTTA E SALMONE
Ravioli with ricotta cheese and smoked salmon

I was sixteen on my first trip to England when I got my first job in the town of Guildford, about 30 miles southwest of London, in a very exclusive Italian restaurant. I can still remember like it was yesterday the flavor and the smell of this beautiful pasta dish. I know you may think it's a bit of effort to prepare, but please believe me, once you've tried it, it will be part of your life forever. Enjoy!

Serves 6
14 ounces fresh egg pasta dough, see page 19
2 eggs, beaten
¾ cup plus 1 tablespoon extra virgin olive oil
3 tablespoons finely chopped fresh chives

For the filling
3 cups ricotta cheese
finely grated zest of 2 lemons
11 ounces smoked salmon, chopped
3 tablespoons finely chopped fresh chives
salt and pepper to taste

1 In a large bowl, mix all the ingredients for the filling together with a fork. Season with salt and pepper. Cover with plastic wrap and let rest in the refrigerator for 10 minutes.

2 Flatten the prepared dough with your fingers so that it can fit through the rollers of the pasta machine. Flour the pasta lightly on both sides and start to roll it from the widest setting to the thinnest. Make sure you keep the pasta dusted with flour at all times.

3 Lay the pasta sheets on a well-floured counter. Place teaspoonfuls of filling at 1¹/2-inch intervals across half the rolled-out dough. Brush the spaces between the fillings with the beaten egg. Gently cover with the other half of the dough and press down between the mounds of filling on all sides.

4 Use a pastry wheel or sharp knife to cut the pasta into squares between the fillings.

5 Cook the ravioli in a large pot of boiling salted water for 3 minutes (work in batches if necessary), drain, and place in the center of a large serving plate. Season with a little salt and pepper.

6 Drizzle with the extra virgin olive oil, sprinkle with the chives, and serve immediately.

PAPPARDELLE DI ZAFFERANO AI FUNGHI
Saffron pappardelle with Marsala and mushrooms

I learned how to make saffron pappardelle in a very famous restaurant in Bologna. Since then, I must have made this recipe at least a hundred times. The earthy flavor of the saffron in the fresh pappardelle is just spectacular, and served with Marsala wine and mushrooms it's at its best. Please make sure you don't overcook the pappardelle.

Serves 4
¼ cup salted butter
4 tablespoons olive oil
2 red onions, peeled and finely chopped
3 cups quartered white mushrooms
salt and pepper to taste
3 tablespoons Marsala wine
⅔ cup heavy cream
2 tablespoons freshly chopped flat-leaf parsley
14 ounces fresh saffron pappardelle, see page 22

1 In a large skillet, melt the butter with the oil over low heat and sauté the onions for 3 minutes, stirring occasionally with a wooden spoon.

2 Add the mushrooms, season with salt and pepper, and cook for an additional 5 minutes, stirring occasionally.

3 Pour in the Marsala wine and cook for another minute to allow the alcohol to evaporate.

4 Pour in the cream with the parsley, stir everything together, and cook for 1 minute more over low heat. Set aside, away from the heat.

5 Meanwhile, cook the pasta in a large pot of boiling salted water until al dente. Drain and return to the same pan.

6 Pour in the mushroom sauce and toss everything together for 30 seconds to allow the flavors to combine.

7 Serve immediately.

RAVIOLI CON CHORIZO PICCANTE
Spicy chorizo and ricotta stuffed ravioli

For some reason I am finding chorizo in our refrigerator every week this year. My wife Jessie loves it in her salads, so I tried to come up with something special for her. I got lots of loving for this one, so I hope it has the same effect for you!

Serves 6

14 ounces fresh egg pasta dough, see page 19
2 eggs, beaten
3/4 cup plus 1 tablespoon extra virgin olive oil

For the filling

5 tablespoons olive oil
11 ounces chorizo, finely chopped
3 medium-hot red chiles, halved, seeded, and finely chopped
3 cups ricotta cheese
3 tablespoons freshly chopped flat-leaf parsley
salt and pepper to taste

1 To prepare the filling, in a small skillet, heat the olive oil over medium heat and sauté the chorizo with the chiles for 2 minutes, stirring occasionally. Set aside and let cool.

2 In a large bowl, mix the cooled chorizo and chiles with the ricotta and parsley using a fork. Season with salt. Cover with plastic wrap and let rest in the refrigerator for 10 minutes.

3 Flatten the prepared dough with your fingers so that it can fit through the rollers of the pasta machine. Flour the pasta lightly on both sides and start to roll it from the widest setting to the thinnest. Make sure you keep the pasta dusted with flour at all times.

4 Lay the pasta sheets on a well-floured counter. Place teaspoonfuls of filling at 1 1/2-inch intervals across half the rolled-out dough. Brush the spaces between the fillings with the beaten egg. Gently cover with the other half of dough. Press down between the mounds of filling.

5 Use a pastry wheel or sharp knife to cut the pasta into squares between the fillings.

6 Cook the ravioli in a large pot of boiling salted water for 3 minutes (work in batches if necessary), then drain, and place in the center of a large serving plate. Season with a little salt.

7 Drizzle with the extra virgin olive oil, sprinkle with plenty of freshly ground black pepper, and serve immediately.

TAGLIATELLE CON SALSICCE E PORCINI
Tagliatelle with sausage, rosemary, and porcini mushrooms

I love good-quality sausage, so this recipe is definitely in my top ten. My grandfather used to make this dish for me when I was a boy, but he used strained tomatoes instead of the cream that I have introduced. I wish he could have tasted my version, as I know I would have gotten a huge cuddle for this one—he would have loved it and I know that you will too. For those of you who don't like mushrooms, you can leave them out—*Buon Appetito!*

Serves 4

14 ounces Italian sausage or good-quality pork
   sausage
6 tablespoons olive oil
1 leek, washed and finely chopped
2 tablespoons finely chopped fresh rosemary leaves
1 2/3 cups dried porcini mushrooms, soaked in warm
   water for 15 minutes and drained
salt and pepper to taste
1/3 cup plus 1 tablespoon dry white wine
2/3 cup heavy cream
18 ounces fresh egg tagliatelle, see page 21

1 Remove the casings from the sausage and place the meat mixture in a bowl.

2 In a large skillet, heat the oil over low heat and sauté the sausage meat and the leek for 5 minutes, stirring occasionally with a wooden spoon to crumble the meat.

3 Add the rosemary and porcini, season with salt and pepper, and cook for an additional 2 minutes.

4 Pour in the wine and cook for another minute to allow the alcohol to evaporate.

5 Pour in the cream, mix everything together, and cook for 1 minute more. Set aside.

6 Meanwhile, cook the pasta in a large pot of boiling salted water until al dente. Drain and return to the same pan.

7 Pour in the cream sauce and toss everything together for 30 seconds to allow the flavors to combine.

8 Serve immediately.

TAGLIATELLE CON CARCIOFI E PROSCIUTTO CRUDO
Tagliatelle with artichokes and prosciutto

Everybody knows that I absolutely love artichokes. I wanted them to feature in at least two or three recipes so you could try them at their best. The inspiration for this dish came from me cutting artichokes in quarters and wrapping them in prosciutto for antipasti. From this I realized that it would be a perfect base to create one of the best recipes in this book. The colors are fantastic and the taste is even better.

Serves 4

6 tablespoons olive oil
2 red onions, peeled and finely sliced
10 slices of prosciutto, cut into strips across the width
10 artichoke hearts in oil, drained and quartered
salt and pepper to taste
1/3 cup plus 1 tablespoon dry white wine
3 tablespoons freshly chopped flat-leaf parsley
14 ounces fresh egg tagliatelle, see page 21
3-ounce piece of Parmesan cheese, shaved

1 In a large skillet, heat the oil over medium heat and sauté the onions and prosciutto for 5 minutes, stirring occasionally with a wooden spoon.

2 Add the artichokes, season with salt and pepper, and cook for an additional 3 minutes, stirring occasionally.

3 Pour in the wine and cook for 1 minute more to allow the alcohol to evaporate. Sprinkle with the parsley, stir everything together, and set aside.

4 Meanwhile, cook the pasta in a large pot of boiling salted water until al dente. Drain and return to the same pan.

5 Pour in the sauce, return the pan to low heat, and toss everything together for 30 seconds to allow the flavors to combine.

6 Divide the pasta among four serving plates, scatter over the Parmesan cheese shavings, and serve immediately.

DRY
PASTA

ORECCHIETTE AI BROCCOLI
Pasta shells with broccoli rabe, chile, and pine nuts

My boys, Luciano and Rocco, absolutely love broccoli. It's by far their favorite vegetable and they would eat it every day if they could. I wanted to give them this dish (without the chile) to see if they'd like it, and honestly, I've never seen them eat so quickly. It was so great giving them an alternative option and I managed to introduce new flavors to them too. This is a really tasty recipe that anyone will love, but if your children like broccoli, it's a definite winner.

Serves 4

8 tablespoons olive oil
11 ounces broccoli rabe, cut into 3/4-inch pieces
2 garlic cloves, finely sliced
6 tablespoons pine nuts
1 medium-hot red chile, seeded and finely sliced
salt to taste
1/3 cup plus 1 tablespoon dry white wine
6 1/2 cups (18 ounces) orecchiette shells
1 1/2 cups freshly grated Parmesan cheese
10 fresh purple basil leaves

1 In a large skillet or wok, heat the oil over medium heat and stir-fry the broccoli, garlic, pine nuts, and chile for 3 minutes, stirring occasionally with a wooden spoon.

2 Season with salt, add the white wine, and cook over medium heat for an additional 8 minutes. Make sure that the broccoli stays al dente.

3 Meanwhile, cook the pasta in a large pot of boiling salted water until al dente. Drain and return to the same pan.

4 Add the broccoli mixture to the pan with the pasta and place the pan over low heat.

5 Sprinkle with the Parmesan cheese and mix everything together for 20 seconds to allow the sauce to coat the pasta evenly.

6 Serve immediately, garnished with the basil leaves.

LINGUINE AL TONNO
Linguine with canned tuna, olives, and chile

Without doubt this has to be one of my father's favorite pasta dishes. I remember when I used to live with him it was a must-have dish at least once a week, but not always with the same shape of pasta. Please make sure you never use tuna in brine for this recipe, and if you like you can add some capers to the sauce.

Serves 4

10 tablespoons extra virgin olive oil
2 garlic cloves, peeled and finely sliced
1/2 cup pitted Kalamata olives, drained and quartered
5 anchovy fillets in oil, drained and chopped
10 cherry tomatoes, quartered
1/2 teaspoon red pepper flakes
1 x 7-ounce can tuna in oil, drained and flaked
2 tablespoons freshly chopped flat-leaf parsley
salt to taste
18 ounces linguine of your choice
4 tablespoons freshly grated cheese

1 In a large skillet, heat the oil over medium heat and sauté the garlic, olives, and anchovies for 1 minute, stirring with a wooden spoon.

2 Add the tomatoes with the chile and cook for an additional 2 minutes.

3 Scatter in the tuna with the parsley, season with a little salt, and mix together for 1 minute. Set aside.

4 Meanwhile, cook the pasta in a large pot of boiling salted water until al dente. Drain and return to the same pan over low heat.

5 Pour in the tuna, tomato, and olive sauce and stir everything together for 30 seconds to allow the flavors to combine.

6 Serve hot, and please don't be tempted to serve it with grated cheese on top.

FUSILLI CON PEPERONI E ZUCCHINE
Fusilli with red bell peppers and zucchini

If you need a quick and impressive recipe with not a lot of washing up to do, this is the one to try. A great pasta dish for a romantic dinner because it's colorful, light, and tasty. The combination of the zucchini, bell peppers, and walnuts is divine, and of course it will all come together with the fresh lemon zest. Perfect for summer barbecues.

Serves 4

2 red bell peppers
2 zucchini, trimmed
5 tablespoons olive oil
pinch of red pepper flakes
4 tablespoons chopped walnuts
salt to taste
5¼ cups (18 ounces) fusilli
finely grated zest of 1 lemon
4 tablespoons freshly grated Pecorino cheese

1 Cut the bell peppers in half lengthwise. Discard the stalk and seeds. Cut into thin slices and then chop into ¹/4-inch cubes.

2 Coarsely shred the zucchini in the center of a clean dish towel and squeeze dry.

3 In a large skillet, heat the oil over medium heat and sauté the bell peppers for 3 minutes, stirring occasionally with a wooden spoon.

4 Add the zucchini, chile flakes, and nuts and cook for an additional 3 minutes, continuing to stir occasionally. Season with salt.

5 Meanwhile, cook the pasta in a large pot of boiling salted water until al dente. Drain and add to the skillet with the sauce.

6 Sprinkle with the lemon zest and stir everything together over medium heat for 30 seconds to allow the flavors to combine.

7 Divide among four serving bowls and serve immediately, topped with the Pecorino cheese.

RIGATONI AI CARCIOFI
Rigatoni with artichokes, garlic, and orange zest

I have always found artichokes a little bit like anchovies — you love them or you hate them! In my case, I absolutely adore them. If you have never tried them, please have a go at this pasta dish—you won't be disappointed. Never ever buy artichokes that are preserved in brine because they aren't worth eating.

Serves 4

2 tablespoons salted butter
6 tablespoons olive oil
2 garlic cloves, peeled and finely chopped
2 tablespoons finely chopped fresh rosemary
1/2 cup pitted Kalamata olives, drained and halved
6 artichoke hearts in oil, drained and cut into quarters
1/3 cup plus 1 tablespoon dry white wine
finely grated zest of 1/2 orange
salt and pepper to taste
7 cups (18 ounces) rigatoni

1 In a large skillet or wok, melt the butter with the oil. Once hot, add the garlic, rosemary, olives, and artichokes and sauté over medium heat for 3 minutes, stirring occasionally with a wooden spoon.

2 Pour in the wine and cook for an additional 2 minutes to allow the alcohol to evaporate.

3 Add the orange zest, season with salt and pepper, and mix everything together. Set aside.

4 Meanwhile, cook the pasta in a large pot of boiling salted water until al dente. Drain and add to the pan with the artichoke mixture.

5 Return the pan to high heat and mix everything together for 30 seconds to allow the sauce to coat the pasta evenly.

6 Serve immediately.

SPAGHETTINI ALL'ARAGOSTA
Spaghettini with lobster and white wine

Often people ask me if I had to choose my last supper what would it be... Well, here it is. I know lobster can be a bit expensive, but the flavor goes a long way and for a special occasion it really makes for a perfect plate of pasta. Substitute the spaghettini with linguine if you want, but please never grate any kind of cheese on top of this dish.

Serves 2

1 whole live lobster, or a ready-cooked one if you prefer, weighing about 2¼ pounds
4 tablespoons extra virgin olive oil
1 garlic clove, peeled and finely sliced
1 small medium-hot red chile, seeded and finely sliced
½ glass of dry white wine
1 tablespoon freshly chopped flat-leaf parsley
1 x 14-ounce can cherry tomatoes, only use half
salt to taste
9 ounces spaghettini

1 To cook the live lobster, bring a large pot of water to the boil and cook the lobster for 10 minutes. Drain and leave to cool.

2 Twist off the claws and pincers, then place on a cutting board. Using the back of a large heavy knife, crack open the large claws. Use a skewer to carefully remove all the meat from the claws and cut into chunks.

3 Place the lobster, back uppermost, on a cutting board and cut in half lengthwise. Remove the meat from the body and cut into chunks. Clean the shell halves under cold running water and set aside.

4 In a large skillet, heat the oil over low heat and sauté the garlic and chile together for about 30 seconds. Add the lobster meat and cook for about 1 minute, stirring with a wooden spoon.

5 Pour in the wine, scatter in the parsley, and cook for an additional minute to allow the alcohol to evaporate.

6 Add the tomatoes, season with salt, and cook, uncovered, for another 3 minutes, stirring occasionally. Set aside.

7 Meanwhile, cook the pasta in a large pot of boiling salted water until al dente. Drain and return to the same pan.

8 Place the pan over low heat and pour in the lobster sauce. Mix everything together for 30 seconds to allow the pasta to absorb the flavors of the lobster sauce.

9 To serve, spoon the pasta into the reserved lobster shells, pour over any remaining sauce, and enjoy.

LINGUINE AL PESTO GENOVESE
Linguine with Genovese basil pesto

In the summer of 2008, I went to visit a friend of mine, Daniele, in the beautiful Ligurian region where basil grows at its best. He introduced me to pesto alla Genovese and I have to admit that since then it's been one of my top pasta recipes to cook at home. Please don't attempt to make pesto with dried basil because it will never work. If you prefer you can substitute the linguine with spaghetti.

Serves 4

1 2/3 cups fresh basil, leaves only
1/3 cup pine nuts
1 garlic clove, peeled
1/2 cup extra virgin olive oil
1/4 cup freshly grated Parmesan cheese
salt and pepper to taste
18 ounces linguine

1 In a food processor, place the basil, pine nuts, and garlic, drizzle in the oil, and blend until smooth.

2 Transfer the basil mixture to a large bowl and fold in the Parmesan cheese. Season with a little salt.

3 Cook the pasta in a large pot of boiling salted water until al dente. Drain and add to the bowl with the pesto.

4 Toss everything together for 30 seconds to allow the pesto to coat the pasta evenly.

5 Serve immediately.

PENNE ALLA TREVISANA
Penne with red endive, sausage, and red wine

A pasta dish designed for a boys' night in watching football. This has great flavors, is very filling, and, most importantly, is very simple to prepare. Make sure you buy good-quality pork sausage, and you can substitute the penne with rigatoni if you wish.

Serves 4
6 ounces good-quality pork sausage
3 tablespoons extra virgin olive oil
1 red onion, peeled and finely chopped
2 whole red endive, washed and shredded
1/3 cup plus 1 tablespoon red wine
18 ounces penne rigate
2 tablespoons heavy cream
2 tablespoons freshly chopped flat-leaf parsley
heaping 1/4 cup freshly grated Parmesan cheese
salt and pepper to taste

1 Remove the meat from the sausage casings.

2 In a large skillet, heat the oil over low heat and sauté the sausage meat and onion for 5 minutes. Stir occasionally with a wooden spoon to allow the meat to crumble.

3 Add the endive, season with salt and pepper, and cook for an additional 1 minute.

4 Pour in the wine and cook for 1 minute more to allow the alcohol to evaporate. Set aside, away from the heat.

5 Meanwhile, cook the pasta in a large pot of boiling salted water until al dente.

6 Once the pasta is ready, return the sauce to medium heat. Drain the pasta and add to the skillet with the sauce.

7 Pour in the cream with the parsley, sprinkle with the Parmesan cheese, and then toss everything together over medium heat for 30 seconds to allow the flavors to combine.

8 Serve immediately.

LINGUINE DI MARE
Seafood linguine with chile and white wine

This is a recipe that you often find in Italian cookery books, but mine will guarantee you minimum effort, maximum satisfaction. This pasta dish has all the flavors of the sea you need, but you won't find yourself in the kitchen cooking for hours. Please make sure your seafood is fresh and if you wish you can substitute the linguine with spaghetti.

Serves 4

9 ounces live clams
9 ounces live mussels
1/3 cup plus 1 tablespoon dry white wine
6 tablespoons extra virgin olive oil
4 garlic cloves, peeled and sliced
1/2 teaspoon red pepper flakes
2 x 14-ounce cans cherry tomatoes
salt to taste
9 ounces cleaned baby squid, quartered
9 ounces raw medium shrimp, peeled
4 tablespoons freshly chopped flat-leaf parsley
18 ounces linguine
finely grated zest of 1 lemon

1 Wash the clams and mussels under cold water and discard any broken ones and those that don't close when tapped firmly.

2 Place in a large saucepan, pour in the wine, cover with the lid, and cook over medium heat for 3 minutes until the shells have opened. Discard any shellfish that remain closed and transfer the rest into a colander placed over a bowl to catch the cooking liquid. Set aside.

3 Heat the oil in the same pan you used for the clams and mussels and gently sauté the garlic until it begins to sizzle. Add the chile and the tomatoes and cook over medium heat for 5 minutes. Season with salt and stir occasionally.

4 Pour 6 tablespoons of the reserved cooking liquid from the shellfish into the sauce and simmer for an additional 2 minutes.

5 Stir in the baby squid and the shrimp and cook for another 3 minutes until the shrimp turn pink.

6 Add the clams, mussels, and the parsley and stir until heated through.

7 Meanwhile, cook the pasta in a large pot of boiling salted water until al dente. Drain and add to the pan with the sauce.

8 Sprinkle with the lemon zest and mix everything together over low heat for 1 minute to allow the sauce to coat the pasta evenly.

9 Serve immediately.

FUSILLI AI FUNGHI E PORRI
Fusilli with crimini mushrooms, leeks, and mascarpone cheese

I must admit this was one of my experiments that I tried one day. I knew the combination of mushrooms, leeks, and garlic would work beautifully and that the mascarpone and chives would work, but all together? It was a gamble, but a gamble that hit the jackpot. The combination is amazing —you are left with a creamy mushroom sauce but with different flavors peeking through with every bite, and it really won't disappoint. You can substitute the fusilli with penne pasta if you wish.

Serves 4

3 tablespoons salted butter
31/2 cups sliced crimini mushrooms
2 leeks, washed and sliced 1/4-inch thick
2 garlic cloves, peeled and finely chopped
1 cup plus 2 tablespoons mascarpone cheese
3 tablespoons freshly chopped chives
4 pinches of cayenne pepper
salt to taste
51/4 cups (18 ounces) fusilli
2/3 cup freshly grated Parmesan cheese

1 In a large skillet, melt the butter over medium heat. Add the mushrooms, leeks, and garlic and sauté for 5 minutes, stirring occasionally with a wooden spoon.

2 Spoon in the mascarpone and cook for an additional minute, stirring continuously. Stir in the chives and cayenne pepper, season with salt, and remove the pan from the heat.

3 Meanwhile, cook the pasta in a large pot of boiling salted water until al dente. Drain and return to the same pan.

4 Pour in the mushroom sauce and stir everything together for 30 seconds to allow the flavors to combine.

5 Divide among four serving plates, sprinkle with the Parmesan cheese, and serve immediately.

PIAZZA
DEL NETTUNO

SPAGHETTINI CON CAPESANTE IN SALSA VERDE

Spaghettini with scallops and parsley pesto

Scallops, parsley, and garlic is a combination made in heaven. This very simple sauce had to be part of my pasta cookbook. This recipe is quick, colorful, and will shout freshness every time you make it. Please don't buy frozen scallops, and never choose curly parsley over the flat-leaf variety. *Buon Appetito!*

Serves 4

3 tablespoons salted butter
9 ounces small shelled scallops
¾ cup fresh flat-leaf parsley, leaves only
⅓ cup pine nuts
2 tablespoons salted capers, rinsed under cold water
1 garlic clove, peeled
½ cup extra virgin olive oil
finely grated zest of 1 lemon
salt and pepper to taste
18 ounces spaghettini

1 In a skillet, melt the butter and cook the scallops for 1 minute on each side (you may want to do this in batches). Set aside.

2 In a food processor, place the parsley, pine nuts, capers, and garlic, drizzle in the oil, and blend until smooth.

3 Transfer the parsley mixture to a large bowl and mix in the scallops and lemon zest. Season with salt and pepper.

4 Meanwhile, cook the pasta in a large pot of boiling salted water until al dente. Drain and add to the bowl with the pesto and scallops.

5 Gently toss everything together for 30 seconds, allowing the pesto to coat the pasta evenly.

6 Serve immediately.

ORECCHIETTE CON CALAMARI E CHORIZO
Pasta shells and beans with squid and chorizo

I absolutely love squid and to me there is no better way to cook it than with a nice spicy chorizo sausage. This is a pasta dish that would be perfect for a party because the flavors and the colors are just amazing. If you prefer you can substitute the parsley leaves with fresh mint, but whatever you do, please make sure you use fresh squid.

Serves 6

scant ½ cup canned chickpeas (garbanzo beans), drained

heaping ½ cup canned borlotti (cranberry) beans, drained

15 cherry tomatoes, quartered

1 medium-hot red chile, seeded and thinly sliced

1 garlic clove, peeled and finely chopped

3 tablespoons freshly chopped flat-leaf parsley

2 tablespoons freshly squeezed lemon juice

8 tablespoons extra virgin olive oil

salt to taste

14 ounces cleaned squid (look for medium-size ones)

3 ounces hot chorizo sausage, thinly sliced

4½ cups (18 ounces) orecchiette shells

1 In a large bowl, combine the chickpeas and borlotti beans with the tomatoes, chile, garlic, and parsley. Pour in the lemon juice and 5 tablespoons of the oil, season with salt, and toss gently together. Set aside.

2 Cut open the body pouch of each squid along one side and use the tip of a small sharp knife to score the inner side into a fine diamond pattern. Then cut each pouch first in half lengthwise and then across into 2 3/4-inch pieces.

3 In a large skillet, heat the remaining oil over high heat and add the squid pieces (scored-side up so they will curl attractively). Also add the tentacles.

4 Sear for about 30 seconds, then turn over and sear for an additional 30 seconds until golden and caramelized. Season with salt, add the chorizo to the pan, and cook for 1 minute more, keeping the heat high. Set aside.

5 Cook the pasta in a large pot of boiling salted water until al dente. Drain and return to the same pan.

6 Return the pan to low heat and pour in the bean mixture, the squid, and the chorizo. Stir everything together for 1 minute to allow the flavors to combine.

7 Serve immediately, and please don't be tempted to serve it with any grated cheese on top.

LINGUINE AVELLINESI
Linguine with smoked salmon and spicy red bell pepper sauce

I learned this recipe from a restaurant situated in the mountains of Avellino in the south of Italy. I remember I was very impressed by the combination of the smoked salmon with the bell peppers, so I have decided to share it with all of you. I have also tried this pasta dish with smoked trout and to be honest it's just as good. Substitute linguine with fettuccine if you prefer and please make sure you use a good-quality white wine.

Serves 4

2 tablespoons salted butter
8 tablespoons olive oil
1 leek, washed and cut into $1/4$-inch slices
1 red bell pepper, halved, seeded. and diced into $1/4$-inch cubes
7 ounces smoked salmon, cut into $1/4$-inch strips
$1/2$ teaspoon red pepper flakes
$1/4$ cup dry white wine
salt to taste
18 ounces linguine
2 tablespoons freshly chopped flat-leaf parsley
finely grated zest of 1 lemon

1 In a large skillet, melt the butter with the oil over medium heat and sauté the leek and bell pepper for 5 minutes, stirring occasionally with a wooden spoon.

2 Add the salmon and the chile and cook for an additional 1 minute. Pour in the wine and cook for 1 minute more to allow the alcohol to evaporate. Season with a little salt and set aside.

3 Meanwhile, cook the pasta in a large pot of boiling salted water until al dente. Drain and return to the same pan.

4 Pour in the salmon and bell pepper sauce along with the parsley and lemon zest. Return to low heat and stir everything together for 30 seconds to allow the flavors to combine.

5 Serve immediately.

PENNE ALL' EMILIANA
Penne with peas, pork, rosemary, and white wine

This recipe comes from the region of Emilia Romagna where pasta dishes are taken very, very seriously. I was there once on holiday and as a souvenir I brought back this beautiful meal. Although I have suggested you use frozen peas, please use fresh ones if they are in season. If you can't find fresh rosemary leaves, don't worry, you can always use fresh thyme leaves instead.

Serves 4

4 tablespoons salted butter
4 tablespoons olive oil
1 pound pork chops, without the bone, cut into ½-inch cubes
1 large onion, peeled and finely chopped
1 tablespoon finely chopped fresh rosemary leaves
salt and pepper to taste
⅔ cup white wine
1 tablespoon tomato paste
¾ cup plus **1** tablespoon warm water
1 ¼ cups frozen peas, defrosted
4⅔ cups (18 ounces) penne rigate
½ cup freshly grated Parmesan cheese

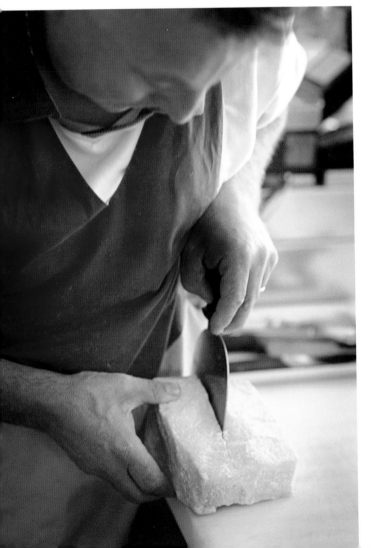

1 In a large skillet, melt the butter with the oil in a large skillet over medium heat and sauté the pork and onion for 5 minutes, stirring occasionally with a wooden spoon, allowing the meat to color on all sides.

2 Add the rosemary, season with salt and pepper, and cook for an additional 1 minute.

3 Pour in the wine and cook for 1 minute more to allow the alcohol to evaporate.

4 Mix in the tomato paste with the warm water and cook over low heat for 40 minutes, stirring occasionally.

5 Add the peas and cook for another 10 minutes, then set aside, away from the heat.

6 Meanwhile, cook the pasta in a large pot of boiling salted water until al dente. Drain and return to the same pan.

7 Pour in the sauce and stir everything together over low heat for 30 seconds to allow the flavors to combine.

8 Serve immediately, sprinkled with the Parmesan cheese.

LINGUINE ALLO ZAFFERANO
Linguine served with a delicate saffron sauce

For me, although this recipe has basic ingredients, it is offering someone something really special. It just oozes flavor and the saffron makes it that much more extravagant. It's like a mixture of an Italian and English carbonara with a twist and it works fantastically. You can substitute the linguine with tagliatelle or spaghetti and the ham with bacon if you prefer, but please leave in the saffron—it really makes the dish.

Serves 4
2 tablespoons salted butter
5 1/2 ounces cooked ham, cut into thin strips
pinch of saffron threads
4 tablespoons water
heaping 1 cup heavy cream
salt and pepper to taste
18 ounces linguine
3 egg yolks
2/3 cup freshly grated Pecorino cheese

1 In a small skillet, melt the butter and gently sauté the ham for 2 minutes. Set aside.

2 Place the saffron in a medium saucepan with the water. Bring to a boil, then remove from the heat and let stand for 5 minutes.

3 Pour the cream into the pan with the saffron and return the pan to the heat. Add the ham and gently simmer for 3 minutes. Season with salt and pepper and set aside.

4 Meanwhile, cook the pasta in a large pot of boiling salted water until al dente. Drain and add to the pan with the saffron sauce.

5 Return the pan to low heat and add the egg yolks, stirring continuously for 10 seconds so they cook in the residual heat.

6 Divide the linguine among four serving plates and serve immediately, topped with the grated Pecorino cheese.

SPAGHETTI POVERACCIO
Spaghetti with anchovies, bread crumbs, and garlic

The word povera means "a poor man" and this is a recipe that was originally created to feed a lot of people with little money, allowing them to make use of inexpensive ingredients. Don't use anchovies marinated in vinegar because they won't work in this dish, but by all means substitute the fresh chile with red pepper flakes. Please, please, please make sure the pasta is cooked al dente.

Serves 4
6 tablespoons olive oil
3 garlic cloves, peeled and halved
8 anchovy fillets in oil, drained and chopped
1 medium-hot red chile, seeded and chopped
heaping 2 cups fresh white bread crumbs
salt to taste
18 ounces spaghetti
3 tablespoons freshly chopped flat-leaf parsley

1 In a skillet, heat the oil over low heat and gently sauté the garlic until golden all over. Remove the garlic and add the anchovies and chile to the oil. Cook for about 3 minutes or until the anchovies have melted into the oil. Set aside.

2 In another skillet, toast the bread crumbs until crispy and golden brown. Set aside.

3 Cook the pasta in a large pot of boiling salted water until al dente. Drain and return to the same pan over low heat.

4 Pour in the anchovy oil, add the parsley and the bread crumbs, and stir everything together for 30 seconds to allow the flavors to combine.

5 Serve immediately.

RIGATONI CON ASPARAGI, PISELLI E FUNGHI

Rigatoni with peas and porcini mushroooms in a creamy asparagus sauce

For anybody who isn't a big fan of rich tomato sauces, this has to be the perfect pasta recipe if you still want bags of flavor on your plate. This dish is so full of fresh ingredients that even though it's in a creamy sauce it doesn't feel heavy. I must admit that every time I make this for a vegetarian they utterly love me—so it must be good.

Serves 4

14 ounces asparagus
4 tablespoons salted butter
1 1/2 cups frozen peas, defrosted
1 cup dried porcini mushrooms, soaked in warm water
   for 15 minutes and drained
2 leeks, washed and cut into 1/4-inch slices
3/4 cup plus 1 tablespoon heavy cream
3 tablespoons freshly chopped flat-leaf parsley
2 pinches of smoked paprika
salt to taste
7 cups (18 ounces) rigatoni
2/3 cup freshly grated Pecorino cheese

1 Use a potato peeler to scrape the asparagus stalks, discarding the woody ends. Chop the stalks into 3/4-inch-long pieces. Drop into a medium saucepan of boiling salted water and cook for 2 minutes. Drain and immediately refresh under cold running water to prevent them from discoloring. Set aside.

2 In a large skillet, melt the butter over medium heat. Add the peas, mushrooms, leeks, and asparagus and sauté for 5 minutes, stirring occasionally with a wooden spoon.

3 Pour in the cream and cook for an additional minute, stirring continuously.

4 Mix in the parsley and paprika, season with salt, and then set aside.

5 Meanwhile, cook the pasta in a large pot of boiling salted water until al dente. Drain and return to the same pan.

6 Pour in the asparagus sauce and stir everything together for 30 seconds to allow the flavors to combine.

7 Divide among four serving plates, sprinkle with the Pecorino cheese, and serve immediately.

SPAGHETTI CON PEPERONI ALLE ERBE
Spaghetti with yellow bell peppers, chile, and herbs

If I was a vegetarian, this is the kind of dish I would eat regularly. I absolutely love bell peppers, especially when you add such fabulous herbs to them. You would think the flavors would overpower each other with three different herbs, chile, and garlic, but I promise you it is a combination that really gets those tastebuds working. You can also use eggplant instead of bell peppers if you like.

Serves 4

8 tablespoons olive oil
2 garlic cloves, peeled and finely sliced
4 yellow bell peppers, seeded and finely sliced
1 teaspoon red pepper flakes
salt to taste
1 teaspoon fresh thyme leaves
1 tablespoon finely chopped fresh rosemary leaves
2 tablespoons finely chopped fresh flat-leaf parsley
18 ounces spaghetti

1 In a large skillet, heat the oil over low heat and gently sauté the garlic and bell peppers for 2 minutes.

2 Add the chile with all the herbs and cook for an additional 6 minutes, stirring occasionally with a wooden spoon. Season with salt and set aside, away from the heat.

3 Meanwhile, cook the pasta in a large pot of boiling salted water until al dente. Drain and return to the same pan.

4 Pour in the bell pepper mixture and stir everything together over low heat for 30 seconds to allow the sauce to coat the pasta evenly.

5 Serve immediately.

BAKED & SWEET PASTA

CANNELLONI DEL NONNO

Cannelloni filled with arugula, spinach, and ricotta cheese

A great baked pasta dish that has been in my family for over twenty years. If you prefer, you can substitute the Pecorino cheese with Parmesan.

Serves 6 to 8

scant 3 cups strained tomatoes
15 fresh basil leaves
salt and pepper to taste
1/3 cup freshly grated Pecorino cheese
14 ounces fresh egg pasta dough, see page 19

For the filling

2 cups ricotta cheese
5 1/2 ounces frozen spinach, defrosted and squeezed
 to remove the excess water
5 1/2 ounces arugula, chopped
1/4 teaspoon freshly grated nutmeg
2/3 cup freshly grated Pecorino cheese

For the béchamel sauce

7 tablespoons salted butter
3/4 cup plus 1 tablespoon all-purpose flour
1 quart cold whole milk
1/4 teaspoon freshly grated nutmeg

1 Preheat the oven to 350°F.

2 Pour the strained tomatoes into a large bowl with the basil leaves. Season with salt and pepper, mix together, and set aside.

3 To prepare the béchamel sauce, in a large saucepan, melt the butter over medium heat. Stir in the flour and cook until it turns light brown in color, 1 minute. Gradually beat in the cold milk, reduce the heat, and cook for 10 minutes, beating continuously. Once thickened, stir in the nutmeg. Season with salt and pepper and set aside to cool slightly.

4 To prepare the filling, in a large bowl, place all the ingredients, season with salt and pepper, and use a fork to mix everything together. Cover with plastic wrap and let rest in the refrigerator while you prepare the pasta.

5 Flatten the prepared dough with your fingers so that it can fit through the rollers of the pasta machine. Flour the pasta lightly on both sides and start to roll it from the widest setting to the thinnest. Cut it into rectangles measuring 2 3/4 x 6 inches—you will need 26 sheets.

6 Prepare a large pot with plenty of boiling salted water and start to cook the pasta sheets—work in batches of five. Boil the sheets for 1 minute, then remove and place immediately in a large bowl of cold water to prevent the pasta from going soggy. After 1 minute in the cold water, remove the sheets and place on a clean dish towel.

7 Place 1 1/2 tablespoons of filling across each pasta sheet and start to roll up the pasta from the narrow side working forward. To seal the cannelloni, overlap the pasta sheet by about 3/4 inch. Repeat until all the pasta sheets are filled.

8 Select a rectangular baking dish measuring 10 x 14 inches and pour in a third of the béchamel sauce. Spread evenly. Place half the cannelloni onto the béchamel layer with the seam facing down. Spoon over half the strained tomatoes and half the remaining béchamel sauce.

9 Build up the second layer of cannelloni and spoon over the remaining strained tomatoes. Spread over the remaining béchamel sauce. Finish by sprinkling over the Pecorino cheese and bake in the center of the oven for 35 minutes or until colored and crispy.

10 Once ready, let rest for 5 minutes out of the oven; it will be easier to cut and serve, as the layers will hold together.

FARFALLE AL SALMONE GRATINATE
Crispy topped farfalle with smoked salmon and chives

If you like smoked salmon and creamy sauces, this recipe will really rock your world. An elegant yet full-of-flavor dish that's got the wow factor. You can use medium-size shells instead of the bow pasta, but please make sure you get your béchamel sauce right—it shouldn't be too runny.

Serves 6

4 1/4 cups (12 ounces) farfalle
1/3 cup salted butter, plus extra for greasing
7 ounces smoked salmon, cut into small strips
3 tablespoons finely chopped fresh chives
1 cup freshly grated Parmesan cheese
salt and pepper to taste

For the béchamel sauce
4 tablespoons salted butter
6 tablespoons all-purpose flour
2 cups cold whole milk
1/2 teaspoon paprika
pinch of freshly grated nutmeg
salt and pepper to taste

1 First make the béchamel sauce. In a large saucepan, melt the butter over medium heat. Stir in the flour and cook until it turns light brown in color, 1 minute. Gradually beat in the cold milk, reduce the heat, and cook for 10 minutes, beating continuously. Once thickened, stir in the paprika and the nutmeg. Season with salt and pepper and set aside to cool slightly.

2 Meanwhile, cook the pasta in a large pot of boiling salted water until al dente. Drain and place in a large bowl with the butter, smoked salmon, chives, half the Parmesan cheese, and half the béchamel sauce. Mix everything together.

3 Preheat the broiler to medium-high. Grease an 8 1/2-inch round ovenproof dish with sides at least 1 1/2 inches deep. Pour the pasta into the dish, cover with the remaining sauce, and sprinkle with the remaining Parmesan cheese.

4 Place the dish under the preheated broiler and cook for 15 minutes until golden and crispy.

5 Once ready, let rest for 5 minutes; it will be easier to cut and serve, as the layers will hold together.

GNOCCHI AL POMODORO
Potato dumplings with tomato sauce and cheddar cheese

When I first met my wife, she told me one of her favorite Italian dishes was Gnocchi al pomodoro. Her mother, Elizabeth, used to make it for her when she was a little girl and they lived in Italy, and every time I make this recipe I can still see those distant memories in her eyes. It is a really homely dish that all the family will love. You can substitute the cheddar for Parmesan cheese if you prefer, and please make sure you don't overcook the gnocchi, otherwise they will become soggy.

Serves 4

4 tablespoons extra virgin olive oil
1 large red onion, peeled and finely chopped
2¾ cups strained tomatoes
10 fresh basil leaves
salt and pepper to taste
18 ounces ready-made plain gnocchi
scant 1 cup freshly grated sharp cheddar cheese

1 Preheat the oven to 400°F.

2 In a medium saucepan, heat the oil and sauté the onion over medium heat until golden, about 3 minutes. Pour in the strained tomatoes and cook for 10 minutes, stirring occasionally with a wooden spoon.

3 Stir in the basil, season with salt and pepper, and set aside, away from the heat.

4 Meanwhile, half-fill a medium saucepan with water, add 1 tablespoon salt, and bring to a boil.

5 Cook the gnocchi in the boiling water, removing them as soon as they start to float to the top. Drain and place in the pan with the sauce. Gently stir everything together to allow the sauce to coat the gnocchi evenly.

6 Transfer to a baking dish. Scatter the cheddar cheese over the top and bake in the center of the oven for 8 minutes until golden and bubbling.

7 Serve immediately.

CONCHIGLIE DI MARE
Shell pasta with shrimp and saffron

Most of my food memories growing up in Naples consist of seafood. We ate it almost every day because we lived by the coast. I've realized that outside Italy many people prefer creamy sauces, so quite often I take traditional recipes and add a little twist for the foreign palate. Please buy fresh shrimp and make sure you only use flat-leaf parsley and not the curly variety.

Serves 6

12 ounces medium shell pasta (look for conchiglie)
$^1/_3$ cup salted butter, plus extra for greasing
11 ounces fresh shrimp, peeled (head and tail removed)
$3^1/_3$ cups fresh baby leaf spinach, washed
4 tablespoons finely chopped fresh flat-leaf parsley
1 cup freshly grated Grana Padano cheese

For the béchamel sauce

4 tablespoons salted butter
6 tablespoons all-purpose flour
2 cups plus 1 tablespoon cold whole milk
4 x 0.125g sachets saffron powder
pinch of freshly grated nutmeg
salt and pepper to taste

1 To prepare the béchamel sauce, in a large saucepan, melt the butter over medium heat. Stir in the flour and cook for 1 minute until it turns light brown in color. Gradually beat in the cold milk, reduce the heat, and cook for 10 minutes, beating continuously. Once thickened, stir in the saffron and nutmeg. Season with salt and pepper and set aside to cool slightly.

2 Meanwhile, cook the pasta in a large pot of boiling salted water until al dente. Drain and place in a large bowl with the butter, shrimp, spinach, parsley, half the Grana Padano cheese, and half the béchamel sauce. Mix everything together to allow the ingredients to coat the pasta evenly. Preheat the broiler to medium-high.

3 Grease an 8$^1/_2$-inch round ovenproof dish with sides at least 1$^1/_2$ inches deep. Pour the pasta into the dish and level the surface. Cover with the remaining béchamel sauce and sprinkle with the remaining cheese.

4 Place the dish under the preheated broiler and cook for 15 minutes until golden and crispy.

5 Once ready, let rest for 5 minutes; it will be easier to cut and serve, as the layers will hold together.

MACCHERONI GRATINATI
Baked pasta with ham and cheese

This is the kind of dish that ticks all the right boxes. You have the crispness of cheesy topping and the sumptuous cheese flavors with the saltiness of the ham and the sweetness of the peas. You won't need a massive portion of this pasta, as it's very heavy, but it is so tasty that you won't be disappointed. What's really great about this recipe is that you can make it in the morning, cover with aluminum foil, and refrigerate it, ready to cook in the evening. You can substitute the Pecorino cheese with Parmesan if you prefer. Perfect served with a glass of cold beer.

Serves 4

1 tablespoon salted butter
11 ounces cooked ham, cut into 1/4-inch cubes
11 ounces macaroni or penne
1 cup heavy cream
scant 1 cup freshly grated Monterey Jack cheese
scant 1 cup freshly grated sharp cheddar cheese
3/4 cup small chunks Gorgonzola cheese
1/4 teaspoon freshly grated nutmeg
2 fresh mozzarella balls, drained and cut into
  1/2-inch cubes
3 egg yolks
heaping 1 cup frozen peas, defrosted
1 cup freshly grated Pecorino cheese
salt and pepper to taste

1 Preheat the oven to 425°F.

2 In a skillet, melt the butter and sauté the ham for 3 minutes until crispy. Set aside.

3 Meanwhile, cook the pasta in a large pot of boiling salted water until al dente. Drain and return to the pan, away from the heat.

4 Pour in the cream with the Monterey Jack, cheddar, and Gorgonzola. Return the pan to low heat and use a wooden spoon to start mixing everything together for 1 minute.

5 Remove the pan from the heat and add the nutmeg, mozzarella, egg yolks, peas, ham, and half the Pecorino cheese. Season with a little salt and plenty of black pepper, and stir together for 30 seconds.

6 Place the pasta into a 12-inch round shallow baking dish, sprinkle with the remaining Pecorino cheese, and bake in the center of the preheated oven for about 15 minutes or until it is bubbling and blistering on top.

7 Once ready, let rest for 5 minutes out of the oven before cutting into servings.

CANNELLONI ALLA MARGHERITA
Cannelloni filled with sun-dried tomatoes, mozzarella, and basil

This dish was inspired by the famous pizza margherita—basically tomato, mozzarella, and basil—fresh ingredients, great colors, and bags of flavor.

Serves 6 to 8

scant 3 cups strained tomatoes
15 fresh basil leaves
14 ounces fresh egg pasta dough, see page 19
1/2 cup freshly grated Parmesan cheese
2 fresh mozzarella balls, drained and finely sliced

For the filling
2 cups ricotta cheese
7 ounces fresh basil leaves, chopped
scant 1 cup sun-dried tomatoes in oil, drained
1/4 teaspoon freshly grated nutmeg
3 fresh mozzarella balls, drained and cut into
　1/2-inch cubes

For the béchamel sauce
7 tablespoons salted butter
3/4 cup plus 1 tablespoon all-purpose flour
1 quart cold whole milk
1/4 teaspoon freshly grated nutmeg
salt and pepper to taste

1 Preheat the oven to 350°F.

2 First make the béchamel sauce following the method described on page 84.

3 In a large bowl, mix the strained tomatoes and basil leaves together, seasoning with salt and pepper.

4 In another large bowl, place all the filling ingredients except the mozzarella, add salt and pepper, and use a fork to mix everything together. Scatter in the mozzarella and fold together. Cover and let rest in the refrigerator.

5 Flatten the prepared dough with your fingers so that it can fit through the rollers of the pasta machine. Flour the pasta lightly on both sides and start to roll it from the widest setting to the thinnest. Cut into rectangles measuring 2 3/4 x 6 inches. You will need 26 sheets.

6 Prepare a large pot with plenty of boiling salted water and start to cook the pasta sheets—work in batches of five. Boil the sheets for 1 minute, then remove and place immediately in a large bowl of cold water to prevent the pasta from going soggy. After 1 minute in the cold water, remove the pasta sheets and place on a clean dish towel.

7 Place 1 1/2 tablespoons of filling across each pasta sheet and start to roll up the pasta from the narrow side working forward. To seal the cannelloni, overlap each pasta sheet by about 3/4 inch. Repeat until all the sheets are filled.

8 Select a rectangular baking dish measuring 10 x 14 inches and pour in a third of the béchamel sauce. Spread evenly. Place half the cannelloni onto the béchamel layer with the seam facing down. Spoon over half the strained tomatoes and half the remaining béchamel sauce.

9 Build up the second layer of cannelloni and spoon over the remaining strained tomatoes. Spread over the remaining béchamel sauce. Finish by sprinkling over the Parmesan cheese and bake in the center of the oven for 20 minutes.

10 Remove the dish from the oven, place the slices of mozzarella on top, and bake for an additional 15 minutes until golden and crispy.

11 Once ready, let rest for 5 minutes out of the oven; it will be easier to cut and serve, as the layers will hold together.

CONCHIGLIONI RIPIENI AL FORNO
Large pasta shells filled with pork and rosemary

Often when you have a party, you look for dishes that you can prepare in advance and then cook at the last minute when your guests arrive. Well—you've just found one. Once you've stuffed the large pasta shells, the only thing left to do is to bake them at the last minute. Substitute the ground pork for lamb or beef if you wish.

Serves 4

24 large pasta shells (look for conchiglioni)
5 tablespoons olive oil
1 onion, peeled and finely chopped
18 ounces ground pork
1 tablespoon finely chopped fresh rosemary leaves
2 x 14-ounce cans chopped tomatoes
15 fresh basil leaves
¾ cup freshly grated Pecorino cheese

For the béchamel sauce
4 tablespoons salted butter
6 tablespoons all-purpose flour
2 cups plus 1 tablespoon cold whole milk
pinch of freshly grated nutmeg
salt and pepper to taste

1 Bring a large pot of salted water to a boil. Parboil the pasta for about 5 minutes, then drain and place the shells, inverted, on a clean dish towel to cool.

2 To prepare the béchamel sauce, in a large saucepan, melt the butter over medium heat. Stir in the flour and cook for 1 minute until it turns light brown in color. Gradually beat in the cold milk, reduce the heat, and cook for 10 minutes, beating continously. Once thickened, stir in the nutmeg. Season with salt and pepper and set aside to cool.

3 In a large skillet, heat the oil over medium heat and cook the onion for 2 minutes until golden.

4 Add the ground pork with the rosemary and stir continuously with a wooden spoon to allow the meat to crumble. Cook for 15 minutes until the meat has browned. Set aside to cool. Preheat the oven to 350°F.

5 Once the pork has cooled, pour half the béchamel sauce into the pan and mix together.

6 Pour the chopped tomatoes into a small saucepan and heat through. When bubbling, add the basil and season with salt and pepper. Cook for 5 minutes.

7 Spread the tomato sauce over the bottom of a 14-x-8-inch ceramic dish—this will prevent the pasta shells from sticking.

8 Using a tablespoon, fill the pasta shells with the pork mixture and gently place in the ceramic dish, making sure the shells aren't too close together. Drizzle the remaining béchamel over each filled shell.

9 Cover with aluminum foil and bake in the center of the oven for 15 minutes. Remove the foil, sprinkle with the Pecorino cheese, and bake for an additional 5 minutes or until the cheese is golden.

10 Once ready, let rest out of the oven for 3 minutes.

11 To serve, spoon some tomato sauce in the center of each plate and arrange six filled pasta shells on top.

PENNE CON ZUCCHINE E SALAME GRATINATE

Crispy topped pasta with zucchini and salami

I designed this recipe one morning when my wife kept mentioning that the food she was going to prepare for a family get-together was a bit boring. She asked me to come up with something more exciting to serve everyone. The only problem was that unfortunately I didn't prepare enough, so my only tip would be, if you try this recipe for a party, make sure you have plenty because your guests will love it. If you do have some left over, you can use it the day after for your lunchbox or a picnic.

Serves 6

6 tablespoons olive oil
2 large zucchini, trimmed and cut into 1/4-inch cubes
salt and pepper to taste
3 1/4 cups (12 ounces) penne rigate
9 ounces salami Milano, cut into small strips
3 tablespoons freshly chopped flat-leaf parsley
1 cup freshly grated Parmesan cheese
butter, for greasing

For the béchamel sauce

4 tablespoons salted butter
6 tablespoons all-purpose flour
2 cups plus 1 tablespoon cold whole milk
1/2 teaspoon paprika
pinch of freshly grated nutmeg

1 In a large skillet, heat the oil over medium heat and sauté the zucchini for 5 minutes, stirring occasionally. Season with salt and pepper, then set aside.

2 To prepare the béchamel sauce, in a large saucepan, melt the butter over medium heat. Stir in the flour and cook for 1 minute until it turns light brown in color. Gradually beat in the cold milk, reduce the heat, and cook for 10 minutes, beating continuously. Once thickened, stir in the paprika and nutmeg. Season with salt and pepper and set aside to cool slightly.

3 Meanwhile, cook the pasta in a large pot of boiling salted water until al dente. Drain and place into a large bowl with the zucchini, salami, parsley, half the Parmesan cheese, and half the béchamel sauce. Gently mix everything together.

4 Preheat the broiler to medium-high. Butter an 8 1/2-inch round ovenproof dish with sides at least 1 1/2 inches deep. Pour the pasta into the dish, cover with the remaining béchamel sauce, and sprinkle with the remaining Parmesan cheese.

5 Place the dish under the preheated broiler and cook for 15 minutes until golden and crispy.

6 Once ready, let rest for 5 minutes; it will be easier to cut and serve, as the layers will hold together.

CANNELLONI TONNO E RICOTTA

Cannelloni filled with tuna, ricotta cheese, and lemon

I love cannelloni but wanted to create a dish that was a bit different from the traditional fillings offered in most cookbooks or restaurants. This filling is so fresh and tasty and yet it has to be the easiest to prepare by far. Only use tuna in oil and not brine, and if you don't have very much time, you can buy the fresh cannelloni tubes ready to be filled, but promise me that you will try and make your own at least once. It's the most satisfying thing in the world and not as hard as you might think.

Serves 4
11 ounces fresh egg pasta dough, see page 19

For the filling
1 cup ricotta cheese
9 ounces canned tuna chunks in oil, drained
finely grated zest of 1/2 lemon
2 tablespoons freshly chopped chives

For the béchamel sauce
heaping 2 tablespoons salted butter
heaping 3 tablespoons all-purpose flour
1 1/4 cups cold whole milk
1/4 teaspoon freshly grated nutmeg
salt and pepper to taste

1 Preheat the oven to 350°F.

2 To prepare the béchamel sauce, in a large saucepan, melt the butter over medium heat. Stir in the flour and cook for 1 minute until it turns light brown in color. Gradually beat in the cold milk, reduce the heat, and cook for 10 minutes, beating continuously. Once thickened, stir in the nutmeg. Season with salt and pepper and set aside to cool slightly.

3 To prepare the filling, in a large bowl, place all the ingredients, season with salt and pepper, and use a fork to mix everything together until smooth. Cover with plastic wrap and let rest in the refrigerator while you prepare the pasta sheets.

4 Flatten the prepared dough with your fingers so that it can fit through the rollers of the pasta machine. Flour the pasta lightly on both sides and start to roll it from the widest setting to the thinnest. Make sure you keep the pasta dusted with flour at all times. Cut into rectangles measuring 2 3/4 x 6 inches. You will need 16 sheets.

5 Prepare a large pot of boiling salted water. Start to cook the pasta sheets, working in batches of four. Boil the sheets for 1 minute, then remove and place in a large bowl of cold water to prevent the pasta from going soggy. After 1 minute in the cold water, remove the pasta sheets and place on a clean dish towel.

6 Place 1 1/2 tablespoons of filling on each pasta sheet and start to roll up the pasta from the narrow side. To seal the cannelloni, overlap each pasta sheet by about 3/4 inch. Repeat until all the pasta sheets are filled.

7 Select a rectangular baking dish measuring about 10 x 14 inches and pour in half the béchamel sauce. Spread evenly over the bottom. Place the cannelloni on the béchamel with the seam facing down. Spread the remaining béchamel sauce over the cannelloni.

8 Cover with aluminum foil and bake in the center of the oven for 15 minutes. Remove the foil and bake for an additional 20 minutes.

9 Once ready, let rest for 5 minutes out of the oven; it will be easier to cut and serve, as the shapes will hold together.

TORTA DI SPAGHETTI E SPINACI
Spaghetti and spinach tart

I love tarts, and considering that I also love pasta, for me there is nothing better than pasta in a tart. I can guarantee you have never seen a recipe like this in any other cookbook, and once you've tried it there will be no going back. If you want, substitute the spinach with arugula and serve with a cold glass of dry white wine.

Serves 8

2 quarts water
salt and pepper to taste
7 ounces spaghetti
5 tablespoons olive oil
2 red onions, peeled and thinly sliced
14 ounces ready-made pie crust
all-purpose flour, for dusting
11 ounces baby leaf spinach, washed and
  coarsely chopped
6 medium eggs
1 cup freshly grated Parmesan cheese

1 Pour the water into a large pot and bring to a boil with 1 tablespoon salt. Cook the pasta in the boiling salted water until al dente. Drain through a colander and rinse under cold running water immediately, to stop the pasta cooking. Once cold, set aside to drain for 5 minutes. Give the pasta a good shake every minute or so.

2 Preheat the oven to 350°F. In a large skillet, heat the olive oil over medium heat and cook the onions, stirring occasionally, until softened, 5 to 6 minutes. Set aside.

3 Roll the pie crust out on a lightly floured counter and use to line a 10-inch loose-bottom tart pan. Chill in the freezer for 10 minutes.

4 Fill the tart pan with parchment paper and pie weights, place on a cookie sheet, and cook in the center of the oven for 15 minutes. Remove the paper and beans and set the tart shell aside to cool.

5 Meanwhile, blanch the spinach by placing it in a colander over the sink and pouring boiling water over it. Squeeze out the excess water and set aside.

6 In a large bowl, lightly beat the eggs. Add the cheese, onions, spinach, and pasta and season with salt and pepper. Mix everything together, then pour into the tart shell, spreading the mixture out evenly.

7 Bake in the center of the oven for about 30 minutes or until the filling is just set. Remove from the oven and let the tart cool in the pan for 15 minutes before removing the pan and transferring the tart to a serving plate.

8 Cut into slices and serve warm or at room temperature with your favorite salad.

TIMBALLO ALLA TORRESE
Baked pasta with meat sauce and Parmesan cheese

This beautiful baked pasta traditionally comes from the town where I was born, Torre del Greco, in the south of Italy. This is where mozzarella comes from and, of course, is used in many recipes. I've used ground beef and pork together because I really believe it gives a better texture to the sauce, and please make sure you also use a good red wine.

Serves 6
4 tablespoons olive oil
1 onion, peeled and finely chopped
1 large carrot, peeled and grated
2 celery stalks, finely chopped
18 ounces ground beef
18 ounces ground pork
salt and pepper to taste

2 glasses of dry red wine
2¾ cups strained tomatoes
2 tablespoons tomato paste
¾ cup plus 1 tablespoon chicken stock
18 ounces fettuccine
3 tablespoons salted butter
4 tablespoons toasted bread crumbs
3 fresh mozzarella balls, drained and sliced
  (don't use buffalo mozzarella)
¾ cup freshly grated Parmesan cheese

1 In a large saucepan, heat the olive oil over medium heat and cook the onion, carrot, and celery for 5 minutes, stirring occasionally with a wooden spoon.

2 Add the ground meats and cook for an additional 5 minutes, stirring continuously until colored all over. Season with salt and pepper.

3 Pour in the red wine, stir well, and cook for another 5 minutes to allow the alcohol to evaporate.

4 Pour in the strained tomatoes with the tomato paste and the stock, lower the heat, and cook, uncovered, for 2 hours, stirring the sauce every 20 minutes.

5 Once the sauce is ready, remove from the heat, season to taste with salt and pepper, and set aside.

6 Cook the pasta in a large pot of boiling salted water until al dente. Drain and return to the same pan. Pour in the meat sauce and gently stir everything together to allow the flavors to combine.

7 Preheat the oven to 350°F. Use some of the butter to grease a 12-inch gratin dish and then sprinkle with the bread crumbs.

8 Spoon half the pasta mixture into the dish and then scatter over the mozzarella cheese. Cover with the remaining pasta.

9 Dot the surface with the remaining butter and sprinkle with the Parmesan cheese.

10 Bake in the center of the oven for 20 minutes until it is bubbling and blistering on top.

11 Before serving, let rest for 5 minutes out of the oven before cutting into servings.

FARFALLE AL CARTOCCIO
Pasta baked with bell peppers and mozzarella

This pasta dish has definitely got the wow factor. Great colors, a fantastic smell, and, most importantly, flavors that are out of this world. Please do not use buffalo mozzarella because it will be too milky and therefore make the pasta soggy. If you prefer you can sprinkle Parmesan cheese over the top once the pasta is ready to be served.

Serves 4

4 quarts water

salt and pepper to taste

4¾ cups (14 ounces) farfalle

5 tablespoons extra virgin olive oil

1 yellow bell pepper, halved, seeded, and chopped into ½-inch cubes

1 red bell pepper, halved, seeded, and chopped into ½-inch cubes

1 garlic clove, peeled and finely sliced

1 lemon

4 tablespoons freshly chopped flat-leaf parsley

2 fresh mozzarella balls, drained and cut into ½-inch pieces

1 Preheat the oven to 400°F. Pour the water into a large pot and bring to a boil with 2 tablespoons salt.

2 Cook the pasta in the boiling salted water until al dente. Drain the pasta through a colander and rinse under cold running water immediately, to stop the pasta cooking. Once cold, set aside to drain for 5 minutes. Give the pasta a good shake every minute or so.

3 In a large skillet, heat the oil and gently sauté the bell peppers with the garlic for 5 minutes, stirring occasionally. Transfer the mixture to a large bowl and set aside to cool.

4 Squeeze over the juice of half the lemon and mix in the pasta and the parsley. Season with salt and pepper.

5 Prepare 4 sheets of aluminum foil, each measuring about 12 x 12 inches.

6 Divide the pasta among the sheets of foil and scatter over the mozzarella. Create a sealed parcel by bringing in the edges and scrunching together. Place on a cookie sheet and bake in the preheated oven for 15 minutes.

7 To serve, place the parcels on serving plates, open, and enjoy immediately.

GNOCCHI ALLA ROMANA CON PROSCIUTTO
Semolina gnocchi with prosciutto

An authentic dish that comes from the region of Lazio and, to be more precise, near the capital of Italy, Rome. It is well known that the Romans make gnocchi with semolina instead of potatoes and that they will only use Pecorino Romano rather than Parmesan cheese. To make the recipe easier to prepare, you can use "quick-cook" semolina instead of the traditional variety, which will take you much longer to cook.

Serves 6

2⅓ cups whole milk
2⅓ cups water
¼ teaspoon freshly grated nutmeg
1¾ cups coarse semolina flour
⅔ cup salted butter
2 cups freshly grated Pecorino Romano cheese
4 eggs, beaten
salt and pepper to taste
6 tablespoons olive oil
2 garlic cloves, peeled and thinly sliced
2 x 14-ounce cans chopped tomatoes
10 fresh basil leaves
12 slices of prosciutto

1 In a large saucepan, combine the milk, water, and nutmeg and bring to a boil.

2 Sprinkle in the semolina with one hand so that it falls like rain into the pan, while beating continuously with a whisk to prevent lumps forming. Continue to beat until the mixture begins to thicken. Change the whisk for a wooden spoon and continue to cook over medium heat for about 10 minutes. The semolina is ready when the mixture begins to come away from the side of the pan.

3 Remove the pan from the heat and mix in a third of the butter, half the cheese, and all the eggs. Season with salt and pepper.

4 Lightly dampen a clean counter with a little cold water and, using a metal spatula, spread out the semolina until it is about ¾ inch thick. Let cool and harden. Meanwhile, preheat the oven to 400°F.

5 Once the semolina has firmed up, use a 2-inch cutter to stamp out circles, reserving the scraps.

6 Use a little of the remaining butter to grease a shallow ovenproof serving dish approximately 14 x 8 inches. Arrange a layer of scraps from the semolina circles on the base of the dish. Lay the semolina circles on top, slightly overlapping.

7 Sprinkle the remaining cheese on top, cut the remaining butter into small pieces, and scatter over the gnocchi. Sprinkle with black pepper and cook in the center of the oven for 30 minutes.

8 Meanwhile, in a large saucepan, heat the olive oil over medium heat and sauté the garlic for 30 seconds. Add the chopped tomatoes and basil and season with salt and pepper. Let the sauce simmer, uncovered, for 15 minutes, stirring occasionally.

9 Once the gnocchi are ready, pour the tomato sauce in the center of a serving dish, some gnocchi on top, and serve immediately with the prosciutto twisted on top.

PENNE E PEPERONATA AL FORNO
Penne with roasted bell peppers and mozzarella

However much effort you put into a vegetarian meal, although tasty, sometimes it can still be a little boring. This dish has it all and offers that special person something a bit more creative. The saltiness of the capers and olives combined with the freshness of the parsley and the creaminess of the mozzarella is a winner every time. It's a really hearty meal and will satisfy everyone—even meat lovers. *Buon Appetito!*

Serves 4

3 tablespoons olive oil
1 garlic clove, peeled and finely sliced
21 ounces roasted peppers (from a can or jar), drained and sliced
1 tablespoon salted capers, rinsed
1/2 cup pitted Kalamata olives, drained
salt and pepper to taste
3 cups (11 1/2 ounces) penne rigate
1 tablespoon freshly chopped flat-leaf parsley
2 fresh mozzarella balls, drained and sliced

1 In a medium saucepan, heat the olive oil and gently sauté the garlic until golden, then add the roasted bell peppers, capers, and olives. Season with salt and pepper, stir, and simmer over medium heat for about 10 minutes, stirring occasionally.

2 Meanwhile, cook the pasta in a large pot of boiling salted water until al dente. Drain and add to the pan with the bell pepper, capers, and olives. Sprinkle with the parsley and mix together.

3 Preheat the broiler to high.

4 Place the pasta mixture in an ovenproof dish measuring about 12 x 6 inches and cover the surface with the mozzarella slices.

5 Grind over some black pepper and place under the preheated broiler for 5 minutes or until the cheese is golden and melted.

6 Serve hot.

MEZZELUNE DOLCI
Half-moon-shape sweet pasta filled with candied fruit

This is a classic Neapolitan dessert that is usually eaten around Easter time. I remember like it was yesterday my grandmother filling the pasta with candied fruits and ricotta cheese and me trying to help her as much as I could, because I knew I'd get an extra serving at the end. You can use good-quality chocolate chips instead of candied fruit.

Serves 6 to 8

3 whole eggs and 2 extra yolks, plus 2 eggs, beaten, for brushing
2 1/3 cups all-purpose flour, plus extra for dusting
4 tablespoons butter, softened
4 tablespoons Amaretto liqueur
1 quart vegetable oil, for deep-frying
confectioners' sugar, for dusting

For the filling
3 tablespoons superfine sugar
1 cup ricotta cheese
finely chopped zest of 1 orange
10 almonds, finely chopped
1 1/2 ounces candied fruit, finely chopped

1 Beat two of the whole eggs in a bowl and set aside.

2 To make the sweet pasta dough, in a food processor, place the remaining one egg and two egg yolks, add the flour, butter, and Amaretto, and process until mixed. Turn out the mixture onto a well-floured counter and knead for 2 minutes until you have a soft dough. Cover with plastic wrap and let rest in the refrigerator for 30 minutes.

3 To prepare the filling, in a medium bowl, mix all the ingredients together with a fork. Cover with plastic wrap and let rest in the refrigerator for 10 minutes

4 Flatten the prepared pasta dough with your fingers so that it can fit through the rollers of the pasta machine. Flour the pasta lightly on both sides and start to roll it

from the widest setting to the thinnest. Make sure you keep the pasta dusted with flour at all times. Lay the pasta sheets on a well-floured counter. Cut into circles using an 3¼-inch cutter—you should get 28 to 30 circles.

5 Place about a teaspoonful of the filling in the center of each circle, sharing it out equally. Brush the edges of the circles with beaten egg and fold over to make half-moon shapes. Press down to seal with your fingertips. Using a fork, press the edges again to secure the filling.

6 In a large saucepan, heat the oil until hot and smoking. Carefully drop in the sweet-filled pasta and deep-fry for about 15 seconds until golden all over. (Be very careful and work in batches—no more than five at a time.)

7 Once cooked, remove the mezzelune using a slotted spoon and place on some paper towels to soak up any excess oil.

8 To serve, place all the mezzelune on a large serving dish and dust with plenty of confectioners' sugar. Serve warm with a little glass of Amaretto or Vin Santo.

PASTICCIO DOLCE
Sweet pasta cake with Amaretto liqueur

With this dessert, a lot of Italians will think I've gone mad. In fact, when I had the boys, Marco, Leo, and Franco, round one night, I made a four-course pasta feast and the dessert was this—they admitted it tasted good, but they laughed for about half an hour over the fact that I was actually making a dessert with pasta. I love it and am sure you will too. Please make sure you let it cool slightly so it sets properly. Use chocolate chips instead of raisins if you prefer.

Serves 6

1 cup raisins
4 tablespoons Amaretto liqueur
3 Granny Smith apples
juice of 1/2 lemon
olive oil, for greasing
salt
9 ounces vermicelli or thin noodle pasta
4 eggs
2/3 cup superfine sugar
1 cup chopped almonds
finely grated zest of 1 orange
4 tablespoons raw brown sugar

1 Place the raisins in a small bowl and pour over the Amaretto. Let soak for 10 minutes.

2 Preheat the oven to 350°F.

3 Peel, core, and coarsely grate the apples. Place in a bowl and squeeze over the lemon juice to prevent the apple from turning brown.

4 Line a 8-x-8-inch loaf pan with parchment paper and lightly brush with oil.

5 Cook the pasta in a large pot of boiling salted water until al dente. Drain and rinse under cold running water. Set aside.

6 Meanwhile, in a large bowl, lightly beat the eggs and superfine sugar together. Add the almonds, orange zest, and raisins with the Amaretto. Fold in the pasta and the grated apples.

7 Pour the mixture into the loaf pan, cover with aluminum foil, and bake for 40 minutes. Remove the foil, sprinkle with the brown sugar, and bake for an additional 10 minutes until lightly browned on top.

8 Remove from the oven and let rest for 15 minutes.

9 Serve at room temperature with a touch of whipped cream.

MEZZELUNE AL CIOCCOLATO
Half-moon-shape pasta filled with chocolate chips and hazelnuts

This is an amazing way of using pasta in a dessert dish. I know it may sound a bit difficult to prepare, but trust me, once you've learned the technique, you will make this dish over and over again. Make sure you never serve this dish hot but always warm or at room temperature, as you will appreciate the flavors more.

Serves 6 to 8
3 eggs and 2 egg yolks, plus 2 eggs, beaten
2 1/3 cups all-purpose flour, plus extra for dusting
4 tablespoons butter, softened
4 tablespoons Grand Marnier
1 quart vegetable oil, for deep-frying
unsweetened cocoa, for dusting

For the filling
3 tablespoons superfine sugar
1 cup ricotta cheese
finely chopped zest of 1/2 orange
12 hazelnuts, finely chopped
1/3 cup finely chopped good-quality semisweet or
   bittersweet chocolate, finely chopped

1 Beat two of the whole eggs in a bowl and set aside.

2 To make the dough, in a food processor, place the remaining whole egg and two egg yolks. Add the flour, butter, and Grand Marnier. Process until the mixture just holds together.

3 Turn the mixture out onto a well-floured counter and knead for 2 minutes until you have a soft dough. Cover with plastic wrap and let rest in the refrigerator for 30 minutes.

4 To prepare the filling, in a medium bowl, mix all the ingredients together with a fork until combined. Cover with plastic wrap and let rest in the refrigerator for 10 minutes.

5 Flatten the prepared dough with your fingers so that it can fit through the rollers of the pasta machine. Flour the pasta lightly on both sides and start to roll it from the widest setting to the thinnest. Make sure you keep the pasta dusted with flour at all times. Lay the sheets on a well-floured counter and cut into circles using a 3 1/4-inch cutter. You should get about 28 to 30 circles in total.

6 Place about a teaspoonful of filling in the center of each circle, sharing it out equally. Brush the edges of the circles with beaten egg and fold over to make half-moon shapes. Press down to seal with your fingertips. Using a fork, press the edges again to secure the filling.

7 In a saucepan, heat the oil until hot and smoking. Carefully drop in the sweet-filled pasta and deep-fry for about 15 seconds until golden all over. (Take great care with the hot oil and don't cook more than five mezzelune at a time).

8 Once cooked, remove the mezzelune using a slotted spoon and place on some paper towels to soak up any excess oil.

9 Place the mezzelune on a large serving dish and dust with cocoa.

10 Serve warm—delicious with a little glass of Vin Santo.

LIKE MAMMA USED TO MAKE

GNOCCHETTI BURRO E SALVIA
Gnocchetti with zucchini in butter and sage sauce

My grandfather, nonno Giovanni, used to be the king of gnocchi. One of my earliest memories as a child is making potato dumplings with him in his kitchen and I really believe that was the start of my love affair with cooking. I know this is a bit challenging, but I promise the effort is worth it and extremely satisfying. Please always use fresh sage and never the dried variety.

Serves 4 as an appetizer or 2 as an entrée

11 ounces russet potatoes, unpeeled
salt and pepper to taste
1 small egg, lightly beaten
¾ cup plus 1 tablespoon all-purpose flour,
  plus extra for dusting
7 tablespoons salted butter
2 medium zucchini, trimmed and cut into ½-inch cubes
1 tablespoon finely sliced fresh sage
⅓ cup freshly grated Parmesan cheese

1 In a large pot, cook the whole potatoes in boiling water for 25 to 30 minutes until tender. Drain well and let cool slightly.

2 Peel the potatoes and press the flesh through a potato ricer into a large bowl. While the potatoes are still warm, add 2 pinches of salt, the egg, and flour. Lightly mix and then turn out onto a floured counter.

3 Knead lightly until you have a soft, slightly sticky dough. (Don't overwork or the gnocchetti will be tough.)

4 Cut the dough in half and then roll each piece into a long sausage shape, about ⅝ inch in diameter. Cut into ¾-inch pieces.

5 Lay the gnocchetti on a lightly floured clean dish towel. Bring a large pot of salted water to a boil. Drop in the gnocchetti and cook for about 2 minutes—they are ready when they float to the surface. Remove from the water with a slotted spoon and let drain.

6 Meanwhile, in a large skillet, melt the butter over medium heat. Once hot, add the zucchini and sauté for 3 minutes before stirring in the sage. Season with salt and pepper and remove from the heat.

7 Transfer the cooked gnocchetti to the skillet and toss everything together.

8 Serve immediately, sprinkled with the Parmesan cheese.

LINGUINE CON GRANCHIO E LIMONE

Linguine with crab, fresh chile, and lemon zest

This is a great pasta dish that I learned in the town of Amalfi approximately twenty years ago, when I had just started catering college. The secret is simple: all the ingredients must be fresh and the pasta has to be al dente. As you know by now, I hate cheese with most fish dishes, so please refrain from adding it.

Serves 4

1 pound cooked, cleaned, and cracked whole crab, in the shell
5 tablespoons extra virgin olive oil
2 garlic cloves, peeled and finely chopped
1 medium-hot red chile, seeded and finely chopped
3 tablespoons freshly chopped flat-leaf parsley
finely grated zest of 1 lemon
3 tablespoons freshly squeezed lemon juice
18 ounces linguine
salt to taste

1 Using a tablespoon, scoop out the crabmeat from the shell and claws into a bowl and mix the white and brown meat together.

2 In a large skillet, heat the oil over low heat and sauté the garlic and chile together for 30 seconds.

3 Add the crabmeat with the parsley and lemon zest and juice. Cook for 1 minute until the crab is heated through. Season with salt and set aside.

4 Meanwhile, cook the pasta in a large pot of boiling salted water until al dente. Drain and return to the same pan, off the heat. Spoon in the crab sauce and stir everything together for 30 seconds to allow the flavors to combine.

5 Serve immediately, and please don't be tempted to serve it with grated cheese on top.

LINGUINE ALLA PUTTANESCA
Linguine with cherry tomatoes, anchovies, and capers

OK guys, this is how it goes... *Puttanesca* in Italian means a dish made by prostitutes. In the old days, when the sailors were coming back to the port of Naples, they were attracted by the local prostitutes who always used to prepare this dish to give them strength before a night of passion. Well, I really think there is nothing more to say—enjoy and I hope the old wives' tale works for you!

Serves 4

6 tablespoons olive oil
1 garlic clove, peeled and finely sliced
8 anchovy fillets in oil, drained and chopped
1/2 teaspoon red pepper flakes
1/4 cup salted capers, rinsed under cold water
1/2 cup pitted Kalamata olives, drained and halved
2 x 14-ounce cans cherry tomatoes
salt to taste
18 ounces linguine

1 In a large skillet or wok, heat the oil over medium heat and sauté the garlic and anchovies for about 2 minutes, stirring occasionally with a wooden spoon. Add the red pepper flakes, capers, and olives and cook for an additional 3 minutes, continuing to stir.

2 Pour in the cherry tomatoes and stir well. Simmer gently for 8 minutes, uncovered, stirring every couple of minutes. Once ready, season with salt, remove from the heat, and set aside.

3 Cook the pasta in a large pot of boiling salted water until al dente. Drain and return to the same pan. Pour in the sauce and stir everything together for 30 seconds to allow the flavors to combine.

4 Serve immediately without any kind of cheese sprinkled on top.

LASAGNE CON PESTO
Lasagna with pesto

I must have tasted at least thirty different lasagna recipes, so believe me when I say that this is the one to try. The fresh basil pesto melted into the béchamel sauce is just *fantastico*.

Serves 6 to 8

3 tablespoons olive oil
1 onion, peeled and finely chopped
1 large carrot, peeled and grated
1 celery stalk, finely chopped
18 ounces ground beef
salt and pepper to taste
1 glass of Italian dry red wine
2³⁄4 cups strained tomatoes
1 tablespoon tomato paste
12 fresh lasagna sheets (each about 4 x 6 inches)
4 tablespoons cold salted butter, cut into ¹⁄2-inch cubes

For the béchamel sauce

7 tablespoons salted butter
³⁄4 cup plus 1 tablespoon all-purpose flour
1 quart cold whole milk
1 cup freshly grated Parmesan cheese
¹⁄4 teaspoon freshly grated nutmeg

For the pesto

1¹⁄3 cups fresh basil leaves
1 garlic clove, peeled
3 tablespoons pine nuts
¹⁄2 cup extra virgin olive oil
¹⁄4 cup freshly grated Parmesan cheese
pinch of salt to taste

1 Preheat the oven to 350°F.

2 To prepare the pesto, in a food processor, place the basil, garlic, and pine nuts. Pour in the oil and blend for about 10 seconds until smooth. Transfer the mixture to a bowl and fold in the cheese. Season with salt and set aside.

3 For the meat sauce, in a large saucepan, heat the olive oil and cook the onion, carrot, and celery for 5 minutes over medium heat. Add the ground beef and cook for an additional 5 minutes, stirring continuously until colored all over. Season with salt and pepper and cook for another 5 minutes, stirring occasionally.

4 Pour in the wine, stir well, and cook for about 3 minutes to allow the alcohol to evaporate. Add the tomatoes and tomato paste, lower the heat, and cook for 1 hour, uncovered, until you get a beautiful rich sauce. Stir occasionally. After about 30 minutes, taste for seasoning.

5 Prepare the béchamel sauce as described on page 84. Once thickened, stir in half the Parmesan cheese, nutmeg, and pesto. Season and set aside to slightly cool.

6 To assemble the lasagna, spread a quarter of the béchamel sauce over the bottom of a deep ovenproof dish measuring about 12 x 10 inches and lay 4 lasagna sheets on top, trimming if necessary to fit the dish. Spread half the meat sauce over the lasagna, then top with a third of the remaining béchamel sauce.

7 Lay 4 more sheets of lasagna on top and cover with the remaining meat sauce. Spread half the remaining béchamel sauce on top. Add a final layer of lasagna and gently spread the rest of the béchamel on top, completely covering all the lasagna sheets. Sprinkle with the remaining Parmesan and scatter over the cubed butter. Grind some black pepper over the whole lasagna.

8 Cook on the bottom rack of the oven for 30 minutes, then place in the center of the oven and increase the temperature to 400°F. Cook for another 15 minutes until golden and crispy all over.

9 Once ready, let rest for 5 minutes; it will be easier to cut and serve, as the layers will hold together.

PENNE ALL' ARRABBIATA
Penne with red chiles, garlic, and chopped tomatoes

This is the kind of pasta I like to prepare when I'm on my own and I'm in need of something quick and tasty to eat. It is the ultimate Italian comfort food; food that satisfies every part of your body. Don't use fresh tomatoes for this sauce otherwise it will be too watery. If you prefer you can use dried chile flakes instead of the fresh chiles.

Serves 4

6 tablespoons extra virgin olive oil
2 garlic cloves, peeled and chopped
2 medium-hot red chiles, seeded and finely chopped
2 x 14-ounce cans chopped tomatoes
3 tablespoons freshly chopped flat-leaf parsley,
  plus extra to serve
salt to taste
4²⁄₃ cups (18 ounces) penne rigate
freshly grated Parmesan cheese, to serve (optional)

1 In a large skillet or wok, heat the oil over medium heat and add the garlic and chile. Sauté for about 1 minute, stirring with a wooden spoon.

2 Pour in the chopped tomatoes and parsley, stir well, and simmer gently, uncovered, for 10 minutes, stirring every couple of minutes.

3 Once ready, season with salt, remove from the heat, and set aside.

4 Meanwhile, cook the pasta in a large pot of boiling salted water until al dente. Drain and return to the same pan.

5 Put the pan back over low heat, pour in the sauce, and stir everything together for 1 minute to allow the flavors to combine .

6 Serve immediately, sprinkled with chopped parsley and grated Parmesan if you wish.

PANZANELLA E PASTA
Northern Italian salad with roasted bell peppers and pasta

Panzanella is a traditional northern Italian salad that is mainly made with bell peppers, tomatoes, salad leaves, and stale bread. My mother once made it into a pasta salad, and although at the time I thought she was going crazy, I have to admit that it was, and still is, *fantastico!* Substitute the penne pasta with fusilli or farfalle if you prefer.

Serves 4

3 red bell peppers
2 tablespoons olive oil, plus extra for drizzling
2 1/3 cups (9 ounces) penne rigate
3 1/2 ounces frisée lettuce, washed
3 1/2 ounces radicchio, washed
1 small cucumber, cut into 1/2-inch cubes
1 large red onion, peeled and finely sliced
3 ripe tomatoes, coarsely chopped
2 tablespoons capers in vinegar, drained
10 fresh basil leaves, coarsely sliced
8 anchovy fillets in oil, drained and chopped

For the dressing
3 tablespoons red wine vinegar
5 tablespoons extra virgin olive oil
1 teaspoon sugar
salt and pepper to taste

1 Preheat the oven to 350°F. Place the whole bell peppers in a large roasting pan and drizzle over the olive oil. Roast for about 20 minutes until the skins are blackened all over. Remove from the oven, place in a large bowl, and cover with plastic wrap. Let rest for 10 minutes.

2 Once the roasted bell peppers have cooled sufficiently to handle, remove the skin, stem, and seeds, then cut the flesh into strips. Set aside.

3 Cook the pasta in a large pot of boiling salted water until al dente. Drain the pasta through a colander and rinse under cold running water immediately, to stop the pasta cooking. Once cold, drizzle with olive oil and set aside to drain for 5 minutes. Give the pasta a good shake every minute or so.

4 In a large bowl, mix the salad leaves, cucumber, onion, tomatoes, capers, basil, and anchovies together. Add the pasta with the bell peppers.

5 In a separate bowl, beat together all the ingredients for the dressing with a fork. Pour the dressing over the pasta salad and gently mix together.

6 Transfer the salad to a large serving dish and serve.

SPAGHETTI CON RICOTTA E PINOLI
Spaghetti with ricotta cheese and toasted pine nuts

This dish isn't what my mamma used to make, but it is a recipe that my friend's mamma made beautifully. Every time I went to his house to play when I was younger, I always begged her to make it for me. It is so full of flavor, and to this day, whenever I eat it, it takes me back to her house around a small kitchen table and reminds me of my childhood.

Serves 4

6 tablespoons pine nuts

1 cup ricotta cheese

½ cup sun-dried tomatoes in oil, drained and cut into thin strips

3 tablespoons finely chopped fresh chives

¼ teaspoon freshly grated nutmeg

10 fresh basil leaves, chopped, plus extra to serve

4 tablespoons extra virgin olive oil

2 tablespoons hot water

salt and pepper to taste

18 ounces spaghetti

1 Heat a dry skillet and toast the pine nuts until they are golden brown all over. Watch carefully, as they burn easily. Set aside.

2 In a large bowl, combine the ricotta, sun-dried tomatoes, chives, nutmeg, basil, and pine nuts. Pour over the oil and the hot water and season with salt and pepper. Mix everything together and let rest at room temperature.

3 Meanwhile, cook the pasta in a large pot of boiling salted water until al dente. Drain and add to the large bowl with the ricotta mixture. Gently fold everything together for 30 seconds to combine the ricotta mixture with the pasta.

4 Serve immediately.

PASTA E FASUL
Spicy pasta with borlotti and cannellini beans

Every time I cook this dish there is only one person in my mind, and that's my mother, Alba. I have to admit that she doesn't have a large recipe collection, but this is by far her signature dish. Whenever I go back to Italy, she will always make me my spicy pasta with beans to remind me of home. If you desire, you can substitute the pasta shells with any small tube-shape pasta, and if you are vegetarian, you can certainly do without the pancetta.

Serves 4

5 tablespoons olive oil
7 ounces pancetta, diced
2 tablespoons freshly chopped rosemary leaves
1/2 teaspoon dried chile flakes
1 x 14-ounce can borlotti beans
2 x 14-ounce cans cannellini beans
2 good-quality vegetable bouillon cubes
1 quart boiling water
11 ounces medium pasta shells (look for conchiglie)
salt to taste

1 In a large saucepan, heat the oil over medium heat and cook the pancetta for 5 minutes, stirring occasionally with a wooden spoon.

2 Add the rosemary and chile flakes and cook for an additional 2 minutes.

3 Pour in the beans with the liquid from the cans, stir everything together, and cook for 5 minutes.

4 Add the bouillon cubes with the boiling water. Stir, lower the heat, and let simmer for 15 minutes with the lid half on. Stir every 5 minutes.

5 Add the pasta to the pan and cook the pasta in the bean sauce over low heat. Season to taste. If the sauce looks too thick, stir in a glass of hot water.

6 Once the pasta is al dente, turn off the heat and let rest for 2 minutes before serving.

7 Divide the pasta among four serving bowls and enjoy with a glass of good red wine.

SPAGHETTI AGLIO, OLIO E PEPERONCINO
Spaghetti with garlic, olive oil, and chile

If you wish to make yourself a really special meal, this is the recipe for you—easy, spicy, and full of flavor.

Serves 4
6 tablespoons extra virgin olive oil
3 garlic cloves, peeled and finely sliced
1 medium-hot red chile, seeded and finely chopped
6 tablespoons freshly chopped flat-leaf parsley
18 ounces spaghetti
salt to taste

1 In a large skillet, heat the oil over low heat and sauté the garlic until golden, about 1 minute.

2 Add the chile and the parsley with 6 tablespoons of the salted water from the pot in which you will cook the pasta. Mix and set aside.

3 Cook the pasta in a large pot with plenty of boiling salted water until al dente. Drain and return to the pan.

4 Pour in chile, garlic, and oil and stir over medium heat for 30 seconds to allow the flavors to combine.

5 Serve immediately without any kind of cheese sprinkled on top.

LINGUINE CON IMPEPATA DI COZZE
Linguine with mussels, garlic, and white wine

There is a little place in the south of Italy called Castellammare where you can find the best and juiciest mussels in the world. The way they prepare them is so simple that I had to share this recipe with you. Make sure you use a good-quality dry white wine and, if you like, you can add a bit of chile. Whatever you do, though, don't put any kind of grated cheese on top.

Serves 4

1 ¾ pounds live mussels
⅔ cup dry white wine
6 tablespoons extra virgin olive oil
2 garlic cloves, peeled and sliced
10 cherry tomatoes, halved
4 tablespoons freshly chopped flat-leaf parsley
salt and pepper to taste
18 ounces linguine

1 Wash the mussels under cold running water, discarding any that are broken and those that don't close when tapped firmly.

2 Place the mussels in a large saucepan, pour over the wine, and cook, covered, over medium heat until they have opened, 5 minutes. Discard any that remain closed. Transfer a colander placed over a bowl to catch the cooking liquid and set aside. Reserve the cooking liquid for later.

3 In the mussel pan, heat the oil and gently sauté the garlic until it begins to sizzle. Add the tomatoes and parsley, then pour in the reserved cooking liquid from the mussels. Cook over medium heat for 2 minutes. Season with salt and plenty of black pepper.

4 Meanwhile, cook the pasta in a large pot of boiling salted water until al dente. Drain and add to the pan with the sauce and the mussels.

5 Gently mix everything together over low heat for 30 seconds to allow the sauce to coat the pasta evenly.

6 Serve immediately.

MINESTRONE ALLA MILANESE
Chunky vegetable and pasta soup

If you like traditional Italian soup, this is the one to have. There are three good things that come from Milan— number one: Veal alla Milanese; number two: Silvio Berlusconi, the Italian prime minister; and finally number three: Minestrone alla Milanese. A chunky vegetable soup that never fails to impress in flavor, look, and ease of preparation. If you prefer, you can do without the pasta but instead serve with some warm crusty bread.

Serves 6

2 carrots, peeled and cut into 1/2-inch cubes
3 celery stalks, cut into 1/2-inch cubes
1 1/2 cups coarsely sliced green cabbage
1 baking potato, peeled and cut into 1/2-inch cubes
2 onions, peeled and coarsely chopped
6 tablespoons extra virgin olive oil
2 quarts vegetable stock, made with 3 good-quality
    vegetable bouillon cubes
2 zucchini, trimmed and cut into 1/2-inch cubes
salt and pepper to taste
11 ounces tiny shell pasta (look for conchigliette)
15 fresh basil leaves
2 garlic cloves, peeled
3/4 cup freshly grated Parmesan cheese

1 In a large saucepan, combine the carrots, celery, cabbage, potato, and onions. Pour in the oil and sauté over medium heat for 3 minutes, stirring occasionally with a wooden spoon.

2 Stir in the stock and, once it starts to boil, add the zucchini. Lower the heat and simmer for 15 minutes. Season to taste with salt and pepper and stir occasionally.

3 Add the pasta and cook, uncovered, until al dente, about 6 minutes, stirring every 2 minutes. Once the pasta is cooked, remove from the heat.

4 In a food processor, place the basil with the garlic, then measure in 8 tablespoons of the hot cooking liquid from the vegetables. Blend to give a smooth runny paste.

5 Pour the basil paste into the pan with the pasta and vegetables. Stir until everything is well combined and check the seasoning.

6 Divide the minestrone among six serving bowls, sprinkle with the Parmesan, and serve immediately.

FUSILLI AI QUATTRO FORMAGGI
Fusilli with four cheeses and chives

If you love cheese, this is the dish for you. I chose very strong-flavored cheeses (all my favorites) and hoped it would work without them overpowering each other, which it does. It will not disappoint you. It is a heavy dish, but so tasty you will find that you still go for seconds. My grandmother used to make it for me and I love the fact that I am now making it for my family and friends. Perfect accompanied with a cold beer.

Serves 4

1 cup whole milk
1 3/4 pounds Gorgonzola cheese, cubed
heaping 2/3 cup grated cheddar cheese
4 tablespoons finely chopped fresh chives
1 teaspoon cayenne pepper
salt to taste
5 1/4 cups (18 ounces) fusilli
1 fresh mozzarella ball, drained and cubed
2/3 cup freshly grated Parmesan cheese

1 Pour the milk into a medium saucepan and add the Gorgonzola and cheddar. Set the pan over medium heat and gently melt the cheeses in the milk, stirring with a wooden spoon.

2 Once the cheeses have melted, add the chives and the cayenne pepper and season with a little salt. Set aside.

3 Cook the pasta in a large pot of boiling salted water until al dente. Drain and then return to the pan over low heat.

4 Pour in the cheese sauce together with the mozzarella and Parmesan. Stir everything together for 30 seconds to allow the flavors to combine and the sauce to thicken.

5 Serve hot.

SPAGHETTI AL POMODORO
Spaghetti with basil and tomato sauce

A pasta dish loved by all, which happens to be my wife's favorite. I try to come up with amazing sauces, and although she likes them all, Jessie will always have this one by choice. My family seem to smother the pasta with Parmesan cheese, the more the better for them, but if the tomatoes are good quality and the basil is fresh, you really need nothing else, and I've yet to meet a child that doesn't like it.

Serves 4

6 tablespoons extra virgin olive oil
1 onion, peeled and finely chopped
2 x 14-ounce cans chopped tomatoes
10 fresh basil leaves
salt and pepper to taste
18 ounces spaghetti

1 In a medium saucepan, heat the oil over low heat and sauté the onion for about 3 minutes until golden, stirring with a wooden spoon.

2 Pour in the tomatoes and basil, season with salt and pepper, and cook, uncovered, over medium heat for 15 minutes, stirring every 5 minutes.

3 Cook the pasta in a large pot of boiling salted water until al dente. Drain and return to the same pan.

4 Pour in the tomato and basil sauce and stir everything together for 30 seconds to allow the flavors to combine.

5 Serve immediately.

CONCHIGLIE RIGATE PICCANTI
Shell pasta with spicy pork and tomato sauce

I love this shape of pasta and this sauce is perfect for it. The delicate taste of the pork with the strong flavors of the chile, olives, and sun-dried tomatoes is a match made in heaven. I know that most people add cheese to pasta sauces, but please don't to this one. It really doesn't need it and will actually ruin the natural flavors of the ingredients. If you fancy, substitute the conchiglie rigate with rigatoni.

Serves 4

5 tablespoons olive oil

1 onion, peeled and finely chopped

scant 1/2 cup pitted Kalamata olives, drained and halved

1 hot red chile, seeded and finely chopped

heaping 1/3 cup sun-dried tomatoes in oil, drained and finely chopped

11 ounces ground pork

1 1/4 cups strained tomatoes

salt to taste

14 ounces medium shell pasta (look for conchiglie rigate)

1 In a medium saucepan or wok, heat the oil over medium heat and sauté the onion and olives for 2 minutes, stirring occasionally with a wooden spoon.

2 Add the chile, sun-dried tomatoes, and ground pork and sauté for 6 minutes, stirring occasionally.

3 Stir in the strained tomatoes, then gently simmer, uncovered, for 5 minutes, stirring every couple of minutes. Season with salt and then set aside, away from the heat.

4 Meanwhile, cook the pasta in a large pot of boiling salted water until al dente. Drain and return to the same pan.

5 Pour in the sauce and stir everything together over low heat for 30 seconds to allow the flavors to combine and the sauce to coat the pasta evenly.

6 Serve immediately without any kind of cheese on top.

SPAGHETTI CON VONGOLE
Spaghetti with clams, garlic, and chile

If you ask me what is a traditional dish from Torre del Greco, the town where I was born, it has to be pasta with clams. Every southern Italian family has their own variation of the recipe, but this is the one I was brought up with and I wouldn't change it for anything else in the world. You can substitute the spaghetti with linguine, but please never, never, never use canned clams—they are disgusting. This is perfect with a glass of cold Prosecco.

Serves 4

1 1/2 pounds live clams
6 tablespoons extra virgin olive oil
2 garlic cloves, peeled and sliced
1/2 teaspoon dried chile flakes
4 tablespoons freshly chopped flat-leaf parsley
salt to taste
18 ounces spaghetti

1 Wash the clams under cold running water, discarding any that are broken and those that don't close when tapped firmly.

2 Place the clams in a large saucepan, cover, and cook over medium heat until they have opened, 3 minutes. Discard any that remain closed. Pour the clams into a colander placed over a bowl and let drain. Reserve the liquid from the clams.

3 In the clam pan, heat the oil and gently sauté the garlic until it begins to sizzle. Add the chile and parsley, then pour in the reserved cooking liquid from the clams. Cook over medium heat for 2 minutes. Season with salt.

4 Meanwhile, cook the pasta in a large pot of boiling salted water until al dente. Drain and add to the pan with the sauce and the clams.

5 Gently mix all the ingredients together over low heat for 30 seconds, allowing the sauce to coat the pasta evenly.

6 Serve immediately.

LINGUINE ALLA AMATRICIANA
Linguine with cherry tomatoes, pancetta, and white wine

With no doubt, I have to dedicate this recipe to my friend and manager, Jeremy Hicks. We have known each other for seven years now and without fail he has to have this pasta dish at least once a week. I actually agree with him—it's one of my favorites too, because I just love the combination of the onion, pancetta, and chile. If you prefer, substitute linguine with spaghetti or tagliatelle.

Serves 4

4 tablespoons olive oil

1 large red onion, peeled and finely sliced

9 ounces pancetta, diced

⅓ cup plus 1 tablespoon dry white wine

2 x 14-ounce cans cherry tomatoes

½ teaspoon dried chile flakes

salt to taste

18 ounces linguine

3 tablespoons freshly chopped flat-leaf parsley

1 cup freshly grated Pecorino Romano cheese

1 In a large skillet or wok, heat the oil over medium heat and sauté the onion for about 5 minutes, stirring occasionally with a wooden spoon. Add the pancetta and cook for an additional 3 minutes. Pour in the wine and cook for 2 minutes more to allow the alcohol to evaporate.

2 Add the cherry tomatoes and chile, stir well, and gently simmer for 8 minutes, uncovered, stirring every couple of minutes. Once the sauce is ready, season with salt, remove from the heat, and set aside.

3 Cook the pasta in a large pot of boiling salted water until al dente. Drain and return to the same pan. Pour in the sauce, add the parsley, and stir everything together for 30 seconds to allow the flavors to combine.

4 Serve immediately, sprinkled with the Pecorino Romano cheese.

BUCATINI ALLA CARBONARA
Bucatini with eggs, pancetta, and Pecorino Romano

This has to be one of my favorite recipes ever, especially with this shape of pasta. Bucatini is like a thick spaghetti with a hole in the middle that runs from one end to the other. This allows the sauce to really coat the pasta inside and out beautifully. If you are a fan of a simple spaghetti dish, I recommend you try this traditional Roman recipe. You can substitute the pancetta with bacon, but please never add cream to this sauce.

Serves 4

9-ounce piece of smoked pancetta
1 tablespoon salted butter
2 tablespoons extra virgin olive oil
4 eggs
4 tablespoons freshly grated Pecorino Romano
4 tablespoons finely chopped fresh flat-leaf parsley
salt and pepper to taste
18 ounces bucatini

1 Cut the pancetta into short strips about ¼-inch wide.

2 In a large skillet or wok, melt the butter with the oil over medium heat and sauté the pancetta until golden and crispy, about 5 minutes. Stir occasionally and, once ready, remove from the heat and set aside.

3 Beat the eggs in a bowl with half the cheese. Add the parsley and plenty of black pepper.

4 Cook the pasta in a large pot of boiling salted water until al dente. Drain and return to the same pan.

5 Add the pancetta and pour in the egg mixture. Mix everything together for 30 seconds with a wooden spoon. (The heat from the pasta will be sufficient to cook the egg to a creamy texture.)

6 Season with salt and pepper and serve immediately with the remaining cheese sprinkled on top.

PASTA ON THE GO

FUSILLI CON GAMBERETTI
Fusilli with shrimp and basil pesto

I love shrimp and usually make a sauce with shrimp, garlic, and arugula, but one night I wanted to use up a half-opened jar of pesto and some tomatoes and came up with this amazing meal. The freshness of the pesto slightly mellowed by the tomatoes, together with the sweet shrimp, makes this the ultimate pasta salad. Of course you can also serve this hot, but it works beautifully for a take-out lunch.

Serves 4
4 quarts water
salt and pepper to taste
4 1/4 cups (14 ounces) fusilli
4 tablespoons olive oil
4 tablespoons good-quality pesto Genovese
  (see page 62)
9 ounces medium shrimp, cooked and peeled
10 cherry tomatoes, halved

1 Measure the water into a large pot and bring to a boil with 3 tablespoons salt. Add the pasta and cook until al dente.

2 Drain the pasta through a colander and rinse under cold running water immediately, to stop the pasta cooking. Once cold, drizzle over the oil and let drain for 5 minutes. Give the pasta a good shake every minute or so.

3 Meanwhile, place all the remaining ingredients in a large bowl.

4 Add the pasta to the bowl and gently mix everything together to allow the flavors to combine.

5 Let the pasta rest at room temperature for 5 minutes, stirring occasionally.

6 Serve immediately or store in a sealed container in the refrigerator for the following day. Don't store longer than 48 hours and always eat at room temperature.

TOFE CON FAGIOLINI E POMODORINI
Shell pasta with green beans and cherry tomatoes

What a great vegetarian dish—full of flavors, colors, and of course, most importantly, very simple to prepare. I sometimes make this pasta when I'm not sure if my guests are vegetarian or not. Even someone who loves meat will like this. Substitute the cherry tomatoes with sun-dried tomatoes, if you like, but make sure you don't use buffalo mozzarella because it will break down and become too runny.

Serves 4

4 quarts water

salt and pepper to taste

18 ounces medium pasta shells (look for tofe, which are about the right size)

2¼ cups trimmed green snap beans, cut into quarters

¾ cup fresh peas (if not in season use frozen ones)

8 tablespoons extra virgin olive oil, plus extra for drizzling

1⅔ cups cherry tomatoes, halved

2 shallots, peeled and sliced into rings

2 fresh mozzarella balls, drained and cut into small cubes

2 tablespoons finely chopped fresh marjoram or oregano leaves

½ cup freshly grated Pecorino cheese

1 Measure the water into a large pot and bring to a boil with 2 tablespoons salt.

2 Cook the pasta with the beans and peas in the salted boiling water until al dente.

3 Drain the pasta, beans, and peas through a colander and rinse under cold running water immediately, to stop the pasta cooking. Once cold, let drain for 5 minutes. Drizzle with a little olive oil and give the pasta a good shake every minute or so.

4 Meanwhile, in a large bowl, place the tomatoes, shallots, mozzarella, and marjoram or oregano. Pour over the extra virgin olive oil, season with salt and pepper, and mix together.

5 Add the pasta, beans, and peas to the bowl, sprinkle with the Pecorino cheese, and gently mix everything together to allow the flavors to combine.

6 Cover with plastic wrap and let rest at room temperature for 15 minutes. Stir every 5 minutes.

7 Serve immediately or keep in a sealed container in the refrigerator for the day after. Don't keep longer than 48 hours and always eat at room temperature.

FRITTATA DI SPAGHETTI
Spaghetti frittata with Parmesan and arugula

When I was fourteen and I got my first scooter, I used to go to the beach with my friends during the summer and my mother always prepared the same brown bag lunch for me—Frittata di Spaghetti. I can still remember the flavors, and no matter how much she made for me, there was never any left over. This dish is even better the day after it's made, once the flavors have developed. You can substitute spaghetti for linguine if you fancy.

Serves 4

11 ounces spaghetti
4 large eggs
5 1/2 ounces arugula, roughly chopped
1/2 cup sun-dried tomatoes in oil, drained
   and chopped
3/4 cup freshly grated Parmesan cheese
salt and pepper to taste
6 tablespoons olive oil

1 In a large pot of boiling salted water, cook the pasta until al dente. Drain into a colander and rinse under cold running water immediately, to stop the pasta cooking. Once cold, let drain for 5 minutes. Give the pasta a good shake every minute or so.

2 Preheat the oven to 350°F.

3 Break the eggs into a large bowl and add the arugula, sun-dried tomatoes, and the grated Parmesan. Season with salt and pepper and mix together.

4 Add the pasta to the egg mixture, mix, and let rest for 5 minutes.

5 Meanwhile, pour the oil in an 8 1/2-inch baking dish with sides about 2 inches deep. Ensure the dish is well coated with oil. Pour in the pasta mixture and then spread it out evenly.

6 Cook in the center of the preheated oven for 20 minutes until crispy and set. Remove from the oven and let rest for 2 minutes before cutting into servings.

7 Serve warm or at room temperature.

CONCHIGLIE CON ZUCCHINE E PANCETTA
Shell pasta with zucchini, garlic, and pancetta

A pasta dish that screams summer every time I make it. I remember whenever I was in Italy and zucchini were in season, my grandfather used to make this dish at least once a week, and if we didn't fancy the sauce with the pasta, we used it to top toasted bread for an appetizer. I still use this zucchini sauce to go on my baked potato with a little sprinkle of grated cheddar on top.

Serves 4

2/3 cup olive oil
3 large zucchini, trimmed and cut into sticks about 1/2 inch wide and 1 1/4 inches long
5 1/2 ounces pancetta, cubed
2 garlic cloves, peeled and halved
2 x 14-ounce cans chopped tomatoes
4 tablespoons freshly chopped flat-leaf parsley
salt and pepper to taste
18 ounces medium shell pasta (look for conchiglie)

1 In a large skillet, heat the oil over medium heat, add the zucchini, and sauté for 5 minutes until golden and crispy on both sides.

2 Use a slotted spoon to remove the zucchini from the pan and drain on paper towels. Sprinkle with a little salt.

3 Discard two-thirds of the oil from the skillet, return to medium heat, and sauté the pancetta with the garlic in the remaining oil for 3 minutes. Stir in the tomatoes and the parsley and simmer for 10 minutes, stirring occasionally with a wooden spoon.

4 Return the zucchini to the pan, stir, and cook for an additional 5 minutes. Season with salt and pepper.

5 Meanwhile, cook the pasta in a large pot of boiling salted water until al dente. Drain and return to the same pan over low heat.

6 Pour in the zucchini sauce and stir everything together for 30 seconds to allow the sauce to coat the pasta evenly.

7 Serve immediately or cool to room temperature, transfer to a sealed container, and store in the refrigerator for the day after. Don't store longer than 48 hours and always eat at room temperature.

FARFALLE CON NOCI E GORGONZOLA
Pasta salad with walnuts and Gorgonzola cheese

Gorgonzola and walnuts have always been a great combination. I find that they work perfectly with pasta and arugula. Of course you can eat this dish hot, but if you are making it for the following day, make sure you eat it at room temperature and mix well before serving. If you prefer, substitute the Gorgonzola with any hard blue cheese of your choice.

Serves 4

4 quarts water
salt and pepper to taste
6 cups (18 ounces) farfalle
8 tablespoons extra virgin olive oil, plus extra for drizzling
9 ounces cold Gorgonzola cheese, cut into
 ½-inch cubes
1 cup walnut halves
7 ounces arugula
2 tablespoons balsamic vinegar

1 Pour the water into a large pot and bring to a boil with 2 tablespoons salt.

2 Cook the pasta in the boiling salted water until al dente. Drain through a colander and rinse under cold running water immediately, to stop the pasta cooking. Once cold, drizzle with oil and let drain for 5 minutes. Give the pasta a good shake every minute or so.

3 Meanwhile, in a large bowl, combine the Gorgonzola, walnuts, and arugula. Pour over the 8 tablespoons extra virgin olive oil and the balsamic vinegar. Season with salt and pepper and mix thoroughly.

4 Add the pasta to the bowl and gently toss everything together to allow the flavors to combine.

5 Cover with plastic wrap and let rest at room temperature for 5 minutes. Stir every 2 minutes.

6 Serve immediately or keep in a sealed container in the refrigerator for the following day. Don't store longer than 48 hours and always eat at room temperature.

PASTIERA DI MACCHERONI
Pasta bake with pancetta, rosemary, and ground pork

In my family, we have to make this pasta dish at least once a week simply because my boys, Luciano and Rocco, absolutely love it. Believe me, although the recipe is for six people, there is never any left over for my chickens. This is not one just for the kids, though—it's the ultimate boys' dinner, which should be accompanied by a good cold beer.

Serves 6

6 tablespoons extra virgin olive oil
1 red onion, peeled and finely chopped
1 carrot, peeled and finely chopped
9 ounces pancetta, cubed
18 ounces ground pork
2 tablespoons freshly chopped rosemary
1 x 14-ounce can cherry tomatoes
salt and pepper to taste
2¾ cups (11 ounces) penne rigate
4 large eggs
½ cup freshly grated Parmesan cheese

1 In a large saucepan, heat 4 tablespoons of the olive oil and sauté the onion and carrot for 5 minutes until soft, stirring occasionally with a wooden spoon.

2 Add the pancetta with the ground pork and rosemary and cook, stirring continuously, until colored all over, about 5 minutes.

3 Pour in the tomatoes, season with salt and pepper, and cook over medium heat for an additional 15 minutes, stirring occasionally. Let cool to room temperature.

4 Meanwhile, cook the pasta in a large pot of boiling salted water until al dente. Drain and add to the meat sauce. Stir well and let cool.

5 Preheat the oven to 350°F.

6 Break the eggs into the pan of cooled pasta and sauce, then add the grated Parmesan. Mix together.

7 Brush the remaining oil over the side and base of an 8½-inch round nonstick baking dish with sides about 2 inches deep. Pour in the pasta mixture and spread out evenly.

8 Cook in the center of the preheated oven for 20 minutes until crispy and set.

9 Once cooked, let rest for 5 minutes—it will be easier to cut and serve, as the layers will hold together. Serve hot or cold.

FUSILLI CON CREMA DI OLIVE
Fusilli with black olive tapenade

A very seasonal southern Italian recipe, which you will find during September and October when the olive harvest takes place. It is great for a picnic and to take to the office, making everybody jealous! If you fancy, you can substitute the parsley with fresh mint.

Serves 4
5¼ cups (18 ounces) fusilli
1¼ cups pitted Kalamata olives, drained
2 garlic cloves, peeled
4 tablespoons salted capers, rinsed and drained
3 tablespoons freshly chopped flat-leaf parsley
5 tablespoons extra virgin olive oil
2 tablespoons freshly squeezed lemon juice

1 Cook the pasta in a large pot of boiling salted water until al dente. Drain through a colander and rinse under cold running water immediately, to stop the pasta cooking. Once cold, let drain for 5 minutes. Give the pasta a good shake every minute or so.

2 Meanwhile, in a food processor, place the olives, garlic, capers, and parsley. Pour in the oil and the lemon juice and start to blend to create a smooth paste. If the tapenade is too dry, add a little cold water to loosen it up. Transfer to a large bowl.

3 Add the pasta to the bowl with the tapenade and gently toss everything together to allow the flavors to combine. Cover with plastic wrap and let rest at room temperature for 15 minutes. Stir every 5 minutes.

4 Serve immediately or transfer to a sealed container and store in the refrigerator for the day after. Don't store longer than 48 hours and always eat at room temperature.

PENNE CON ZUCCHINE E SALMONE
Penne with zucchini, smoked salmon, and lemon zest

This dish is excellent if you are not keen on fishy flavors. I know it works because my wife Jessie doesn't really like any kind of fish and yet this is one of her favorite recipes.

Serves 2
2 zucchini, trimmed
5 tablespoons olive oil
1/2 teaspoon red pepper flakes
2 tablespoons pine nuts
5 1/2 ounces smoked salmon, coarsely chopped
salt to taste
2 1/3 cups (9 ounces) penne rigate
finely grated zest of 1/2 lemon
2 tablespoons finely chopped fresh chives

1 Coarsely grate the zucchini and place in the center of a clean dish towel. Squeeze over a sink, allowing all the water from the zucchini to run out.

2 In a large skillet, heat the oil over medium heat and sauté the zucchini for 3 minutes, stirring continuously to ensure they cook evenly. Add the red pepper flakes, pine nuts, and smoked salmon and cook for a further 5 minutes. Season with salt and set aside.

3 Meanwhile, cook the pasta in a large pot of boiling salted water until al dente. Drain and return to the same pan.

4 Add the zucchini mixture to the pasta with the lemon zest and chives and toss everything together over medium heat for 30 seconds.

5 Serve immediately or cool to room temperature, transfer to a sealed container, and store in the refrigerator for the day after. Don't store longer than 48 hours and always eat at room temperature.

RIGATONI CON MELANZANE E POMODORINI
Rigatoni with eggplant, garlic, and cherry tomatoes

I know many of you are scared of eggplant, but please trust me when I say this is the easiest and yet the most beautiful recipe to make. The flavor of the fried eggplants with the cherry tomatoes is absolutely divine. This is a fantastic dish to use for dinner parties. It is important to use only fresh basil leaves, as dried ones will ruin the dish.

Serves 4

2 medium eggplants, trimmed
2/3 cup olive oil
salt and pepper to taste
3 garlic cloves, peeled and halved
2 x 14-ounce cans cherry tomatoes
10 fresh basil leaves
7 cups (18 ounces) rigatoni

1 On a cutting board, cut the eggplants in half lengthwise, then into quarters, and then sticks about 1/2 inch wide, discarding the center part containing the seeds.

2 In a large skillet, heat the oil, add the eggplant, and sauté until golden brown and crispy, about 5 minutes.

3 Use a slotted spoon to remove the eggplant from the pan and drain on paper towels. Sprinkle with a little salt.

4 Discard two-thirds of the oil from the pan and sauté the garlic in the remaining oil for 30 seconds. Add the tomatoes and basil, stir everything together, and simmer over medium heat for 10 minutes, stirring occasionally.

5 Return the eggplant to the pan, stir, and cook for an additional 5 minutes. Season with salt and pepper and set aside.

6 Cook the pasta in a large pot of boiling salted water until al dente. Drain and return to the same pan.

7 Return the pan to low heat, pour in the sauce, and stir everything together for 30 seconds to allow the flavors to combine.

8 Serve immediately or cool to room temperature, transfer to a sealed container, and store in the refrigerator for the following day. Don't keep longer than 48 hours and always eat at room temperature.

FARFALLINE TONNO E FAGIOLI
Three bean and tuna pasta salad

I used to make this recipe without the pasta. Tuna and bean salad is amazing all year round. I was having a few friends round for lunch once and wanted to make lots of different dishes. I tried adding farfalline to the tuna salad to make it a more substantial meal and it was a massive hit. It's such a tasty dish and not only extremely healthy but hugely filling too!

Serves 6

4 quarts water
2⅔ cups (11 ounces) farfalline
1 x 14-ounce can chickpeas (garbanzo beans), drained
1 x 14-ounce can red kidney beans, drained
1 x 14-ounce can lima beans, drained
2 x 7-ounce cans tuna in oil, drained
1 red onion, peeled and finely sliced
1 lemon
6 tablespoons extra virgin olive oil
2 tablespoons freshly chopped mint leaves
salt and pepper to taste

1 Pour the water into a large pot and bring to a boil with 2 tablespoons salt. Cook the pasta in the boiling salted water until al dente. Drain through a colander and rinse under cold running water immediately, to stop the pasta cooking. Once cold, let drain for 5 minutes. Give the pasta a good shake every minute or so.

2 In a large bowl, place all the beans with the tuna and the sliced onion. Squeeze over the juice of half the lemon and pour in the oil. Add in the mint and season with salt and pepper. Mix everything together and let rest for 5 minutes at room temperature.

3 Add the pasta to the bowl with the beans and gently toss everything together to allow the flavors to combine. Cover with plastic wrap and let rest at room temperature for 15 minutes. Stir every 5 minutes.

4 Serve the pasta immediately or transfer to a sealed container and store in the refrigerator for the day after. Don't store longer than 48 hours and always eat at room temperature.

PENNE ALLA CRUDAIOLA

Penne with feta cheese, cherry tomatoes, and mint

If you are in a rush and need to prepare something quickly, putting this plate of pasta together couldn't be simpler. I have taken the concept of a traditional Italian sauce, but just by changing the type of cheese and adding mint, this dish becomes extremely fresh, light, and yet still filling. The feta and mint are a fantastic Mediterranean combination and this recipe will not disappoint you.

Serves 4

5 tablespoons extra virgin olive oil
1 garlic clove, peeled and finely sliced
2 cups cherry tomatoes, halved
salt and pepper to taste
3¾ cups (14 ounces) penne rigate
10 fresh mint leaves, finely sliced
1¼ cups cubed feta cheese

1 In a skillet, heat the oil and gently sauté the garlic and cherry tomatoes for 1 minute, stirring with a wooden spoon. Season with salt and pepper and set aside, away from the heat.

2 Meanwhile, cook the pasta in a large pot of boiling salted water until al dente. Drain and return to the same pan.

3 Pour in the garlic and tomatoes and add the mint and feta cheese. Toss everything together, away from the heat, for 30 seconds to allow the flavors to combine.

4 Serve immediately or cool to room temperature, transfer to a sealed container, and store in the refrigerator for the following day. Don't store longer than 48 hours and always eat at room temperature.

CONCHIGLIE ALLA CAPRESE
Shell pasta with tomato, mozzarella, and fresh basil

Back to simple yet perfect combinations—the traditional, but never tired, mozzarella, basil, and tomato. It just shouts fresh, tasty, and Italian. Try and buy the freshest cherry tomatoes you possibly can, and buffalo mozzarella is best for this dish. If you prefer, you can substitute the shell pasta with fusilli or farfalle.

Serves 4

20 cherry tomatoes, halved
15 fresh basil leaves
3 fresh mozzarella balls, drained and cut into
  1/2-inch cubes
4 quarts water
8 tablespoons extra virgin olive oil
salt and pepper to taste
14 ounces medium shell pasta (look for conchiglie)

1 In a large bowl, place the tomatoes, basil, and mozzarella. Drizzle over the oil and season with salt and pepper. Mix and set aside while you cook the pasta.

2 Measure the water into a large pot and bring to a boil with 3 tablespoons salt. Cook the pasta in the boiling salted water until al dente. Drain through a colander and rinse under cold running water immediately, to stop the pasta cooking. Once cold, let drain for 5 minutes. Give the pasta a good shake every minute or so.

3 Add the pasta to the bowl with the tomato mixture and then gently mix everything together to allow the flavors to combine.

4 Let rest at room temperature for 10 minutes, stirring every couple of minutes.

5 Serve immediately or cool to room temperature, transfer to a sealed container, and store in the refrigerator for the day after. Don't store longer than 48 hours and always eat at room temperature.

PENNE ALLA CALABRESE
Penne with cherry tomatoes, garlic, olives, and capers

When I was a boy, I used to go to camping with my family in Calabria and this plate of pasta is what I remember most from those fun days. The secret is very simple: fresh and good-quality ingredients. Don't try and use dried basil, as it spoils the dish. If you prefer, you can substitute the pitted black olives with green ones.

Serves 4

4 tablespoons extra virgin olive oil
1 2/3 cups cherry tomatoes, quartered
2 tablespoons salted capers, rinsed under cold water
2 garlic cloves, peeled and finely chopped
10 pitted Kalamata olives, chopped
3 tablespoons pine nuts
1/2 cup sun-dried tomatoes in oil, drained and
   cut into strips
salt and pepper to taste
4 2/3 cups (18 ounces) penne
10 fresh basil leaves

1 In a large skillet, heat the oil over medium heat and gently sauté the cherry tomatoes for 1 minute, stirring with a wooden spoon.

2 Add the capers, garlic, olives, pine nuts, and sun-dried tomatoes. Sauté for an additional 3 minutes, stirring continuously. Season with salt and pepper and set aside.

3 Meanwhile, cook the pasta in a large pot of boiling salted water until al dente. Drain and return to the same pan.

4 Pour in the sauce with the basil and stir everything together for 30 seconds to allow the flavors to combine.

5 Serve immediately or cool to room temperature, transfer to a sealed container, and store in the refrigerator for the following day. Don't store longer than 48 hours and always eat at room temperature.

FUSILLI CON ZUCCHINE ALLA SCAPECE
Pasta salad with zucchini and balsamic vinegar

If I had to choose one thing I have in common with my father, it would have to be our love of this dish. We both adore zucchini and are both big fans of balsamic vinegar. A little tip for you—you can also use the zucchin sauce as a topping for bruschetta.

Serves 4

4¼ cups (14 ounces) fusilli
5 tablespoons extra virgin olive oil, plus extra for drizzling
2 large zucchini, trimmed
3 tablespoons balsamic vinegar
2 garlic cloves, peeled and thinly sliced
15 fresh mint leaves
salt and pepper to taste
¾ cup cubed feta cheese

1 Cook the pasta in a large pot of boiling salted water until al dente. Drain through a colander and rinse under cold running water immediately, to stop the pasta cooking. Once cold, drizzle with olive oil and let drain for 5 minutes. Give the pasta a good shake every minute or so.

2 Meanwhile, cut the zucchini in half lengthwise and then slice into ¼-inch-thick semicircles.

3 In a large skillet, heat the 5 tablespoons olive oil over medium heat and sauté the zucchini for 5 minutes, stirring occasionally. Splash with the balsamic vinegar, add the garlic, and cook for 1 minute more.

4 Scatter the mint over the zucchini, season with salt and pepper, and mix all together. Set aside to cool.

5 Place the pasta in a large bowl with the zucchini mixture and feta cheese. Gently mix everything together to allow the flavors to combine. Let rest at room temperature for 5 minutes. Stir occasionally.

6 Once ready, serve the pasta immediately or store in a sealed container in the refrigerator for the day after. Don't store longer than 48 hours and always eat at room temperature.

FARFALLE CON FAVE E PROSCIUTTO
Farfalle with fava beans and ham

A traditional Roman recipe that never fails to impress. You can substitute the cooked ham with Parma ham or speck, but never use buffalo mozzarella, as it will release far too much milk and completely ruin the look of the dish. If you leave out the pasta, it also makes a great side salad to accompany any meat.

Serves 4

4 quarts water
6 cups (18 ounces) farfalle
1 ¾ cups shelled fava beans
8 tablespoons extra virgin olive oil, plus extra for drizzling
¾ cups coarsely chopped walnuts
1 ½ cups diced cooked ham
1 ⅓ cups cherry tomatoes, halved
2 fresh mozzarella balls, drained and cut into small cubes
  (don't use buffalo mozzarella)
3 tablespoons freshly chopped flat-leaf parsley
salt and pepper to taste

1 Pour the water into a large pot and bring to a boil with 3 tablespoons salt. Cook the pasta with the fava beans in the boiling salted water until al dente. Drain the pasta and beans through a colander and rinse under cold running water immediately, to stop the pasta cooking. Once cold, let drain for 5 minutes. Drizzle with a little olive oil and give a good shake to the pasta every minute or so.

2 Meanwhile, in a large bowl, place the walnuts, ham, tomatoes, mozzarella, and parsley. Pour over the extra virgin olive oil, season with salt and pepper, and gently mix together.

3 Add the pasta with the fava beans to the bowl and gently toss together to allow the flavors to combine.

4 Cover with plastic wrap and let rest at room temperature for 15 minutes. Stir every 5 minutes.

5 Serve immediately or store in a sealed container in the refrigerator for the day after. Don't store longer than 48 hours and always eat at room temperature.

RIGATONI AL PESTO ROSSO

Rigatoni with sun-dried tomato and basil pesto

If you are a fan of traditional tomato and basil sauce, then you will love this recipe. The flavors are similar, but the sun-dried tomatoes and Pecorino cheese are stronger in both smell and taste. People will feel you are being extravagant, when really the three ingredients are very similar to the basic Neapolitan sauce—this dish is just the posh version!

Serves 4

4 quarts water
7 cups (18 ounces) rigatoni
15 fresh basil leaves
1 ¼ cups sun-dried tomatoes in oil, drained and oil reserved
extra virgin olive oil, as required
½ cup freshly grated Pecorino cheese
salt and pepper to taste

1 Pour the water into a large pot and bring to a boil with 2 tablespoons salt. Cook the pasta in the boiling salted water until al dente. Drain through a colander and rinse under cold running water immediately, to stop the pasta cooking. Once cold, let drain for 5 minutes. Give the pasta a good shake every minute or so.

2 Meanwhile, in a food processor, place the basil and the sun-dried tomatoes with their reserved oil and blend to a smooth paste. If the paste is too dry, add a little extra virgin olive oil to loosen it up.

3 Pour the tomato paste into a large bowl, fold in the Pecorino cheese, and season with black pepper.

4 Add the pasta to the bowl and gently mix everything together to allow the flavors to combine. Cover with plastic wrap and let rest at room temperature for 15 minutes. Stir every 5 minutes.

5 Serve the pasta immediately or transfer to a sealed container and store in the refrigerator for the following day. Don't store longer than 48 hours and always eat at room temperature.

PASTA FOR THOSE WITH ALLERGIES

PAPPARDELLE ALLA BOSCAIOLA
Pappardelle with ham, mushrooms, and cream
▶ EGG, FISH, AND NUT FREE

In Naples where I come from, we don't often use cream in our pasta sauces, maybe because it's too hot or maybe instead because we tend to use cheese to get that creamy texture. When I arrived in England and found cream, I loved experimenting with it. I wanted to create a fresh sauce, which the parsley, tomatoes, and ham give you, but make it softer on the palate. I love this dish and it's so easy to make.

Serves 4
4 tablespoons olive oil
1 large white onion, finely sliced
2 cups diced cooked ham
2¾ cups sliced crimini mushrooms
2 x 14-ounce cans cherry tomatoes
⅓ cup plus 1 tablespoon heavy cream
salt and pepper to taste
18 ounces pappardelle
3 tablespoons freshly chopped flat-leaf parsley
1 cup freshly grated Parmesan cheese

1 In a large skillet or wok, heat the oil over medium heat and sauté the onion for about 5 minutes, stirring occasionally with a wooden spoon. Add the ham and mushrooms and cook for an additional 3 minutes.

2 Pour in the cherry tomatoes and stir well. Simmer gently, uncovered, for 8 minutes, stirring every couple of minutes. Pour in the cream and season with salt and pepper. Mix everything together, then remove from the heat and set aside.

3 Meanwhile, cook the pasta in a large pot of boiling salted water until al dente. Drain and return to the same pan. Pour in the Boscaiola sauce with the parsley and stir everything together for 30 seconds to allow the flavors to combine.

4 Serve immediately with the freshly grated Parmesan cheese sprinkled on top.

ZUPPA DI CIPOLLE E PASTINA
Onion and pancetta soup with pasta
▶ EGG, FISH, AND NUT FREE

This recipe originally featured in my last book (*The Italian Diet*) as a soup dish. I had such amazing feedback that I have decided to turn it into a pasta soup. Believe you me, if you haven't tried this yet you are missing out—this is the ultimate comfort food.

Serves 4

5 1/2 ounces pancetta or bacon slices

5 tablespoons extra virgin olive oil

1 1/2 pounds white onions, peeled and finely sliced

scant 2 quarts chicken stock, made with 3 good-quality chicken bouillon cubes

1 x 14-ounce can chopped tomatoes

salt and pepper to taste

7 ounces tiny pasta shells (look for conchigliette or lumachine)

6 fresh basil leaves, shredded

4 tablespoons freshly grated Pecorino or Parmesan cheese

1 Cut the pancetta or bacon into 1/4-inch pieces and place in a large saucepan. Place the pan over medium heat and start to sauté the pancetta or bacon for 2 minutes, stirring continuously.

2 Pour in the oil with the onions and stir everything together. Lower the heat and cook for 20 minutes, stirring occasionally, to allow the onions to take on a beautiful golden color.

3 Once the onions are colored, pour in the chicken stock and chopped tomatoes. Season to taste with salt and pepper and bring to a boil. Lower the heat, half-cover with a lid, and simmer for 20 minutes, stirring occasionally.

4 Add the pasta and cook, uncovered, over a low heat until al dente, about 6 minutes, stirring every 2 minutes.

5 Once the pasta is cooked, remove the pan from the heat and stir in the basil and the cheese.

6 Serve immediately with some warm crusty bread.

PENNE CON SALSICCIA E RUCOLA

Penne with Italian sausage and arugula

▶ GLUTEN, EGG, FISH, AND NUT FREE

For everyone looking for a quick yet very tasty pasta dish, this is definitely the one to try. I absolutely love the combination of sausage, garlic, and fennel seeds—it gives you the ultimate Italian flavors. If you can't find Italian sausage, try any good-quality sausage, but please make sure it has a very high meat content.

Serves 4

7 ounces Italian sausage (check it's gluten free)
5 tablespoons extra virgin olive oil
1 garlic clove, peeled and thinly sliced
1 teaspoon fennel seeds
salt to taste
1/2 glass of dry white wine
4 2/3 cups (18 ounces) gluten-free penne rigate
1 cup freshly grated Pecorino cheese
3 1/2 ounces arugula

1 Remove the casings from the sausage and place the meat in a bowl.

2 In a large skillet, heat the oil over low heat and sauté the sausage meat and the garlic for 3 minutes. Stir occasionally with a wooden spoon, allowing the meat to crumble.

3 Add the fennel seeds, season with salt, and cook for an additional minute.

4 Pour in the wine and cook for 1 minute more. Set aside, away from the heat.

5 Meanwhile, cook the pasta in a large pot of salted boiling water until al dente.

6 Once the pasta is cooked, return the sauce to medium heat. Drain the pasta and tip into the pan with the sauce.

7 Sprinkle with the Pecorino cheese and arugula and toss everything together over medium heat for 30 seconds to allow the flavors to combine.

8 Serve immediately.

SPAGHETTI AL GORGONZOLA
Spaghetti with Gorgonzola and white wine sauce

▶ GLUTEN, EGG, FISH, MEAT, AND NUT FREE

If you are watching your weight, don't make this one! It tastes amazing and the butter, wine, cream, and Gorgonzola make it worth eating, but I can't lie to you and try to give you healthy alternatives, as this dish has to be left alone. Although you might think it's heavy—trust me, you will finish your serving and still want more. If it helps, I can confirm that you will lose 105 calories for every 30 minutes of bedroom action, so enjoy both!

Serves 4

2 tablespoons salted butter
7 ounces Gorgonzola cheese, cut into chunks
2/3 cup heavy cream
3 tablespoons dry white wine
2 tablespoons freshly chopped flat-leaf parsley
1/2 teaspoon smoked paprika
salt to taste
18 ounces gluten-free spaghetti

1 In a medium saucepan, melt the butter over low heat. Add the Gorgonzola and cook, stirring with a wooden spoon, until melted, 2 minutes.

2 Pour in the cream and white wine and cook for an additional 1 minute, stirring continuously, to allow the alcohol to evaporate.

3 Mix in the parsley and paprika, season with salt, and then set aside.

4 Cook the pasta in a large pot of boiling salted water until al dente. Drain and tip back into the same pan.

5 Pour in the Gorgonzola sauce and stir everything together for 30 seconds to allow the flavors to combine.

6 Serve immediately.

FUSILLI AL PESTO E YOGURT
Fusilli with basil pesto, lemon zest, and yogurt
▶ EGG, MEAT, AND FISH FREE

For anyone who is not very keen on basil pesto because it's too strong a flavor, this is a good alternative. By using Greek yogurt it makes the pesto smoother. Substitute the fusilli with farfalle if you prefer, and please use a good-quality extra virgin olive oil.

Serves 4

2 cups fresh basil, leaves only
1/3 cup pine nuts
1 garlic clove, peeled
1/2 cup extra virgin olive oil
finely grated zest of 1 lemon
heaping 1/3 cup Greek-style yogurt
salt and pepper to taste
5 1/4 cups (18 ounces) whole-wheat fusilli

1 In a food processor, place the basil, pine nuts, and garlic. Drizzle in the oil and blend until smooth.

2 Transfer the basil mixture to a large bowl and fold in the lemon zest and yogurt. Season with salt and pepper and set aside.

3 Cook the pasta in a large pot of boiling salted water until al dente. Drain and tip into the bowl with the yogurt pesto. Toss everything together for 30 seconds to allow the pesto to coat the pasta evenly.

4 Serve immediately.

RIGATONI AL PECORINO SARDO
Rigatoni with soft cheese and Pecorino Sardo
▶ MEAT, FISH, AND NUT FREE

In the summer of 2007, I spent a whole month on the island of Sardinia with my family. That is where my love affair with Pecorino Sardo cheese started. On the way back to London, I bought so much of the cheese that I used it in all sorts of combinations, but this is by far my favorite. A smooth plate of pasta with a great punchy flavor.

Serves 4

4 tablespoons salted butter
heaping 1 cup soft cream cheese, e.g. Philadelphia
3 tablespoons whole milk
8 fresh basil leaves, finely chopped
1 cup freshly grated Pecorino Sardo
salt and pepper to taste
5 1/2 cups (14 ounces) whole-wheat rigatoni

1 In a medium saucepan, melt the butter in a saucepan over low heat.

2 Tip in the cream cheese with the milk, basil, and Pecorino cheese and cook for 1 minute, stirring continuously. Season with a little salt and plenty of black pepper. Remove from the heat and set aside.

3 Meanwhile, cook the pasta in a large pot of boiling salted water until al dente. Drain and tip back into the same pan.

4 Pour in the cheese sauce and stir everything together for 30 seconds to allow the sauce to coat the pasta evenly.

5 Serve immediately.

CONCHIGLIETTE CON PISELLI, CAROTE E PANCETTA
Shell pasta with peas, carrots, pancetta, and chile
▶ GLUTEN, FISH, AND NUT FREE

Is it soup? Is it pasta? It's both. A brilliant combination of a fresh vegetable broth, but with the kick of pancetta and chile. Adding the shell-shape pasta finishes off this dish perfectly, making it extremely filling and tasty, yet it's still so easy to prepare—the ultimate one-pot dish. It can be eaten in smaller servings as an appetizer or as an entrée.

Serves 4

5 tablespoons olive oil
1 large red onion, peeled and finely chopped
2 large carrots, peeled and diced about the size of a pea
9 ounces pancetta, diced to the size of a pea
1 1/2 cups frozen peas, defrosted
1 teaspoon red pepper flakes
1 quart vegetable stock, made with 2 good-quality vegetable bouillon cubes (check they are gluten free)
9 ounces tiny shell gluten-free pasta
2 eggs
1 cup freshly grated Parmesan cheese
salt to taste

1 In a large saucepan, heat the oil over medium heat and sauté the onion and carrots until golden, about 5 minutes. Add the pancetta and sauté for an additional 2 minutes, stirring occasionally with a wooden spoon.

2 Add the peas and red pepper flakes and cook for another 3 minutes, stirring occasionally.

3 Pour in the stock, lower the heat, and let simmer for 15 minutes with the lid half on.

4 Remove the lid and add the pasta. Stir well and cook over low heat, uncovered, until the pasta starts to soften, about 8 minutes. Stir every 2 minutes.

5 Once the pasta is cooked al dente, remove the pan from the heat.

6 Crack in the eggs and mix for 30 seconds, allowing the broth to thicken.

7 Finally, add the Parmesan cheese, check whether a little salt is needed, and stir well. Serve immediately.

SPAGHETTI CON PESTO ALLA SICILIANA

Spaghetti with Sicilian pesto

▶ EGG, FISH, AND MEAT FREE

This is a recipe that you will find in every cookbook in Italy, but mine will guarantee maximum satisfaction. Never use dry-packed sun-dried tomatoes because they will be too salty, but you can substitute the almonds with pine nuts if you prefer. Honestly, for this dish you can really use any shape of pasta you wish—enjoy!

Serves 4

1/3 cup whole blanched almonds
20 medium fresh basil leaves, plus extra to serve
3/4 cup sun-dried tomatoes in oil, drained
4 garlic cloves, peeled and halved
extra virgin olive oil, as required
3/4 cup freshly grated Parmesan cheese
salt and pepper to taste
18 ounces whole-wheat spaghetti

1 In a dry skillet, toast the almonds over medium heat until golden brown all over. Set aside to cool.

2 In a food processor, place the basil and sun-dried tomatoes with the garlic. As you start to blend, pour in enough extra virgin olive oil to create a smooth paste.

3 Add the almonds and continue to blend until creamy. Add more oil if necessary.

4 Transfer the mixture to a large bowl and use a fork to fold in the Parmesan cheese. Season with salt and pepper and set aside.

5 Cook the pasta in a large pot of boiling salted water until al dente. Drain well and add to the bowl with the pesto. Mix everything together for 30 seconds to allow the pesto to coat the spaghetti.

6 Serve the spaghetti immediately, with a few basil leaves scattered over the top.

DITALINI ALLA CREMA VERDE
Ditalini with spinach and Parmesan cheese
▶ EGG, FISH, MEAT, AND NUT FREE

For anyone who loves spinach, this is the dish for you. As you can see from the ingredients, there are very few items to buy and yet the flavor is amazing. I have tried this recipe with arugula instead of spinach and it works just as well. Please make sure you use fresh rather than frozen spinach.

Serves 4

2 tablespoons salted butter
1 onion, peeled and finely chopped
7 cups fresh spinach leaves, washed
1/3 cup plus 1 tablespoon hot vegetable stock
12 ounces ditalini
salt and pepper to taste
2/3 cup freshly grated Parmesan cheese

1 In a medium saucepan, melt the butter over low heat and sauté the onion until golden, about 3 minutes, stirring with a wooden spoon.

2 Add the spinach to the pan with the stock and cook, uncovered, over medium heat for 10 minutes, stirring every 2 to 3 minutes.

3 Meanwhile, cook the pasta in a large pot of boiling salted water for 2 minutes less than the package directions. Drain and add to the pan with the spinach. Cook the pasta for an additional 2 minutes with the spinach to allow the flavors to combine. Season with salt and pepper and stir occasionally.

4 Serve hot, topped with the grated Parmesan cheese.

LINGUINE CON CIPOLLE E ACCIUGHE
Linguine with sautéed red onions and anchovies

▶ GLUTEN, EGG, MEAT, AND NUT FREE

If you love anchovies and you fancy something full of flavor, this is a really exciting dish to try. It's colorful and extremely easy to prepare. Use anchovies preserved in oil rather than those marinated in vinegar. If you prefer you can substitute the linguine with spaghetti.

Serves 4

$\frac{1}{3}$ cup salted butter
18 ounces red onions, peeled and finely sliced
$\frac{2}{3}$ cup warm water
3$\frac{1}{2}$ ounces anchovies in oil, drained and chopped
3 tablespoons freshly chopped flat-leaf parsley
18 ounces gluten-free linguine
salt and pepper to taste

1 In a medium saucepan, melt the butter over medium heat and sauté the onions for 5 minutes, stirring occasionally with a wooden spoon.

2 Pour in the warm water and cook for an additional 40 minutes, stirring every 5 minutes.

3 Stir in the anchovies and cook until they have completely dissolved, about 5 minutes. Sprinkle with the parsley and set aside, away from the heat.

4 Meanwhile, cook the pasta in a large pot of boiling salted water until al dente. Drain and return to the same pan.

5 Pour in the onion and anchovy sauce and stir everything together over low heat for 30 seconds to allow the flavors to combine. Season to taste with a little salt and pepper.

6 Serve immediately.

FUSILLI ALLA PIZZAIOLA ▸ GLUTEN, EGG, DAIRY, FISH, MEAT, AND NUT FREE
Fusilli with garlic, chopped tomatoes, and oregano

I like this recipe because you can also use the sauce to accompany broiled or grilled chicken or fish. This pasta will take you a little over ten minutes to prepare and will make you feel really satisfied.

Serves 4
6 tablespoons extra virgin olive oil
3 garlic cloves, peeled and finely sliced
2 x 14-ounce cans chopped tomatoes
10 pitted Kalamata olives, halved
2 teaspoons dried oregano (or fresh if you have some)
salt and pepper to taste
5¼ cups (18 ounces) gluten-free fusilli

1 In a large skillet, heat the oil over medium heat and sauté the sliced garlic for about 1 minute, stirring with a wooden spoon.

2 Pour in the chopped tomatoes with the olives and oregano. Stir and then gently simmer, uncovered, for 10 minutes, stirring every couple of minutes.

3 Once ready, season with salt and pepper, remove from the heat, and set aside.

4 Meanwhile, cook the pasta in a large pot of boiling salted water until al dente. Drain and tip back into the same pan.

5 Return the pan to low heat, pour in the Pizzaiola sauce, and stir everything together for 30 seconds to allow the flavors to combine.

6 Serve immediately—without any kind of cheese on top.

PASTA E ZUCCA ▶ MEAT, FISH, AND NUT FREE
Pasta soup with pumpkin, eggs, and cheddar cheese

A typical winter soup in the D'Acampo family, always eaten one or two days after Halloween. There are so many carved pumpkins around our house that I had to come up with a recipe to try and eat some of them!

Serves 4

4 tablespoons olive oil

1 large white onion, peeled and finely chopped

2⅔ cups cubed, peeled and seeded pumpkin

2 quarts hot vegetable stock, made with 3 good-quality vegetable bouillon cubes

salt and pepper to taste

9 ounces medium shell pasta (look for conchiglie)

3 eggs

½ cup grated cheddar cheese

3 tablespoons freshly chopped flat-leaf parsley

1 In a large saucepan, heat the oil over medium heat and sauté the onion until golden, about 5 minutes. Add the pumpkin and sauté for an additinal 2 minutes. Stir occasionally with a wooden spoon.

2 Pour in the stock, lower the heat, and let simmer for 15 minutes with the lid half on.

3 Remove the lid and season with salt and pepper. Add the pasta and cook, uncovered, over low heat, for about 6 minutes more. Stir every 2 minutes.

5 Once the pasta is cooked, remove the pan from the heat. Crack in the eggs and mix everything together for 30 seconds to allow the broth to thicken.

7 Stir in the cheddar and serve immediately, sprinkled with the parsley.

PENNE AL MASCARPONE E PANCETTA

Penne with mascarpone, pancetta, and Parmesan

▶ GLUTEN, EGG, FISH, AND NUT FREE

Eggplants are an amazing vegetable that often get forgotten. The flavors of the pancetta, Parmesan cheese, parsley, and eggplant are fabulous on their own, but adding in the mascarpone gives the perfect creamy texture without any heaviness. You can substitute the Parmesan for Pecorino cheese and the pancetta for bacon if you prefer.

Serves 4

2 tablespoons olive oil
1 tablespoon salted butter
9 ounces pancetta, cubed
1 medium eggplant, trimmed and cut into
  1/2-inch cubes
1 cup plus 2 tablespoons mascarpone cheese
salt and pepper to taste
4²/₃ cups (18 ounces) gluten-free penne rigate
4 tablespoons finely chopped flat-leaf parsley
4 tablespoons freshly grated Parmesan cheese

1 In a large skillet or wok, heat the oil and butter over medium heat and add the pancetta and eggplant. Sauté, stirring occasionally with a wooden spoon, until golden and crispy, about 5 minutes.

2 Add the mascarpone cheese, stir everything to combine, and cook for an additional 2 minutes. Season with salt and pepper. Remove from the heat and set aside.

3 Cook the pasta in a large pot of boiling salted water until al dente. Drain and tip back into the same pan, off the heat. Stir in the mascarpone sauce with the parsley and the Parmesan cheese.

4 Mix everything together for 30 seconds to allow the sauce to coat the pasta evenly.

5 Serve immediately.

ZUPPA DI PASTA CON PATATE E PORRI
Pasta soup with potatoes, pancetta, and leeks

▶ EGG, FISH, AND NUT FREE

Many people would never associate pasta and potato, but in this case you are really going to have to trust me. This recipe has been in my family for over fifty years, and considering that so far there have been two chefs in the family, it must be *fantastico*! Make sure you use a mealy potato like a Russet, and you can substitute pancetta with bacon if you wish.

Serves 4

6 tablespoons olive oil
1 large leek, washed and finely chopped
9 ounces pancetta, cubed
1 large carrot, peeled and cut into 1/4-inch cubes
14 ounces mealy potatoes, peeled and cut into 1/2-inch cubes
2 quarts hot vegetable stock, made with 3 good-quality vegetable bouillon cubes
3 tablespoons canned chopped tomatoes
salt and pepper to taste
2 1/4 cups (9 ounces) farfalline
2/3 cup freshly grated Parmesan cheese

1 In a large saucepan, heat the olive oil over medium heat and sauté the leek and pancetta for about 3 minutes. Add the carrot and potato and sauté for another 2 minutes. Stir occasionally with a wooden spoon.

2 Pour in the stock, lower the heat, and let simmer, uncovered, for 20 minutes.

3 Mix in the chopped tomatoes and season to taste with salt and pepper.

4 Add the pasta and cook, uncovered, over low heat until al dente, about 6 minutes. Stir every 2 minutes.

5 Once the pasta is cooked, remove the pan from the heat and stir in the Parmesan cheese.

6 Serve immediately with some warm crusty bread.

PASTA E CAVOLFIORE
Shell pasta with cauliflower, eggs, and Parmesan cheese
► GLUTEN, FISH, AND NUT FREE

When I first described this dish to my family, they thought I was mad. They couldn't understand how the combination of flavors would taste nice and I'm happy to say that now they admit defeat. They loved it and now I have to make it at least a couple of times a month, even more in the winter. It is such a homey dish and couldn't be easier to prepare, yet will leave you completely satisfied. Try it and see!

Serves 4

5 tablespoons olive oil
1 large white onion, peeled and finely chopped
2½ cups cauliflower florets, coarsely chopped
2 quarts hot chicken stock, made with 3 good-quality chicken bouillon cubes
salt and pepper to taste
11 ounces medium gluten-free shell pasta (look for conchiglie)
3 eggs
1 cup freshly grated Parmesan cheese

1 In a large saucepan, heat the oil over medium heat and sauté the onion until golden, 3 to 5 minutes. Add the cauliflower and sauté for an additional 2 minutes, stirring occasionally with a wooden spoon.

2 Pour in the stock, lower the heat, and let simmer for 15 minutes with the lid half on.

3 Remove the lid, season with salt and pepper, and add the pasta. Cook, uncovered, over low heat until the pasta is al dente, about 8 minutes, stirring every 2 minutes.

4 Remove from the heat, crack in the eggs, and mix everything together for 30 seconds to thicken the broth.

5 Finally, add the Parmesan cheese and stir well, then serve immediately.

PENNE IN SALSA ROSA

Penne served in a pink tomato and cream sauce

▶ GLUTEN, EGG, FISH, MEAT, AND NUT FREE

This recipe reminds me of my boys, as it was their first real pasta dish. The cream makes the tomato and basil sauce much milder on the palate, and of course it will be a big hit with little girls because the sauce is pink. It is a really easy dish to make and is perfect for a small child being introduced to new flavors. Substitute the penne with spaghetti if you prefer.

Serves 4

6 tablespoons extra virgin olive oil
1 onion, finely chopped
2¾ cups strained tomatoes
10 fresh basil leaves
salt and white pepper to taste
⅓ cup plus 1 tablespoon heavy cream
4⅔ cups (18 ounces) gluten-free penne rigate

1 In a medium saucepan, heat the oil over low heat and sauté the onion until golden, 3 to 5 minutes, stirring with a wooden spoon.

2 Pour in the strained tomates, add the basil, and season with salt and pepper. Cook, uncovered, over medium heat for 10 minutes, stirring every 2 to 3 minutes.

3 Pour in the cream and cook for an additional 5 minutes.

4 Meanwhile, cook the pasta in a large pot of boiling salted water until al dente. Drain and tip back into the same pan. Pour in the tomato and cream sauce and stir everything together for 30 seconds to allow the flavors to combine.

5 Serve immediately.

INDEX